Y0-EGF-615

PREACHING TRUTHS FOR PERILOUS TIMES

Carl G. Johnson

BAKER BOOK HOUSE
Grand Rapids, Michigan

CONTENTS

PREFACE

I have just completed twenty-five years in the ministry of the Lord Jesus Christ—fourteen years as a pastor, and eleven years as an evangelist. As I have preached "the unsearchable riches of Christ" throughout the eastern part of the United States and in two foreign countries, God has blessed this ministry. I say with the apostle Paul, "And I thank Christ Jesus our Lord, who hath enabled me, for that he counted me faithful, putting me into the ministry."

In this book I share sermon outlines, which God has given me, with others who preach the Word of God. Many ministers have said they want more "meat" on the "skeleton" of sermon outlines which they use as aids in their sermon preparation. I have given more than bare outlines, and my prayer is that God may be pleased to use these outlines in the lives of those who read them and use them, as well as in the lives of those who hear them preached. I want ministers to feel free to use anything in this book for the glory of God, "that God in all things may be glorified through Jesus Christ, to whom be praise and dominion for ever and ever. Amen."

Writing in *Moody Monthly,* Warren W. Wiersbe said: "Frances Bacon, in one of his essays, compares students to spiders, ants, and bees, and we may justly apply the illustration to preachers. Some preachers never study, but, like the spider, spin everything out from within, beautiful webs that never last. Some are like ants that steal whatever they find, store it away, and use it later. But the bee sets the example for us all: he takes from many flowers, but he makes his own honey."

Preachers, don't "spin everything out from within" or "steal whatever [you] find," but take "from many flowers" and make your "own honey."

1

A CHARGE TO THE PREACHER

I Timothy 4:16
Acts 20:28

It has been said about preachers:

> If the pastor is young, they say he lacks experience; if his hair is grey, then he's too old for the young people.

> If he has five or six children, he has too many; if he has no children, then they say he's setting a bad example.

> If he preaches from his notes, he has canned sermons and is too dry; if his messages are extemporaneous, he is not deep.

> If he is attentive to the poor people in the church, they claim he is playing to the grandstand; if he pays attention to the wealthy, he is trying to be an aristocrat.

> If he uses too many illustrations, he neglects the Bible; if he doesn't use enough illustrations, he isn't clear.

> If he condemns wrong, he's cranky; if he doesn't preach against sin, he's a compromiser.

> If he preaches the truth, he's offensive; if he doesn't preach the truth, then he's a hypocrite.

> If he fails to please everybody, he's hurting the church and ought to leave; if he does please everybody, he has no convictions.

> If he preaches tithing, he's a moneygrabber; if he doesn't preach Scriptural giving, he is failing to develop his people.

> If he drives an old car, he shames his congregation; if he drives a new car, then he is setting his affection upon earthly things.

If he preaches all the time, the people get tired of hearing one man; if he invites guest preachers, he's shirking his responsibility. If he receives a large salary, he's mercenary; if he receives only a small salary, well—it proves he isn't worth much anyway.

God's Word gives a threefold charge to the preacher.

I. "Take heed unto thyself."

God says to the preacher in I Timothy 4:16: "Take heed unto thyself. . . ." Richard Baxter explained:

Take heed to yourselves, because the tempter (the devil) will make his first and sharpest onset upon you. . . . Oh, what a conquest will he think he hath got, if he can make a minister lazy and unfaithful; if he can tempt a minister into covetousness or scandal. He will glory against the church, and say, "These are your holy preachers: you see what their preciseness is, and whither it will bring them." He will glory against Jesus Christ Himself, and say, "These are Thy champions! I can make Thy chiefest servants to abuse Thee; I can make the stewards of Thy house unfaithful. "

Robert Murray McCheyne wrote to a preacher friend:

Do not forget the culture of the inner man—I mean of the heart. . . . Remember you are God's sword, His instrument—I trust, a chosen vessel unto Him to bear His name. In great measure, according to the purity and perfection of the instrument, will be the success. It is not great talents God blesses, so much as likeness to Jesus. A holy minister is an awful weapon in the hand of God.

Charles H. Spurgeon, the prince of preachers, gave very good advice to preachers.

When we say to you, my dear brethren, take care of your life, we mean be careful of even the smallest detail of your character. Avoid little debts, unpunctuality, gossiping, nicknaming, petty quarrels, and all other of those little vices which fill the ointment with flies. The self-indulgences which have lowered the repute of many must not be tolerated by us. The familiarities which have laid others under suspicion, we must chastely avoid. The roughnesses which have rendered some obnoxious . . . we must put away. We cannot afford to run great risks through little things. Our care must be to act on the rule, "giving no offence in anything, that the ministry be not blamed."

A preacher should be:

A. A man of purity. ". . . Be ye clean, that bear the vessels of the Lord" (Isa. 52:11).

B. A man of prayer. "But we will give ourselves continually to prayer, and to the ministry of the word" (Acts 6:4).

C. A man of preparation. "Study to shew thyself approved unto God, a workman that needeth not to be ashamed, rightly dividing the word of truth" (II Tim. 2:15).

D. A man of power. "But ye shall receive power, after that the Holy Ghost is come upon you: and ye shall be witnesses unto me both in Jerusalem, and in all Judaea, and in Samaria, and unto the uttermost part of the earth" (Acts 1:8).

Spurgeon summarizes the charge to the preacher:

If we do not have the Spirit of God, it were better to shut the churches, to nail up the doors, to put a black cross on them, and say, "God have mercy on us!" If you ministers have not the Spirit of God, you had better not preach, and you people had better stay at home. I think I speak not too strongly when I say that a church in the land without the Spirit of God is rather a curse than a blessing.

II. "Take heed . . . unto the doctrine."

A. Sound doctrine. "But speak thou the things which become sound doctrine" (Titus 2:1).

B. Profitable doctrine. ". . . I kept back nothing that was profitable unto you. . . ." (Acts 20:20).

C. Complete doctrine. "For I have not shunned to declare unto you all the counsel of God" (Acts 20:27).

III. "Take heed . . . to all the flock."

Paul exhorted the preachers who came to him: "Take heed therefore unto yourselves, and to all the flock. . . ." (Acts 20:28).

A. Feed them. "Feed the church of God" (Acts 20:28). Peter charged: "Feed the flock of God which is among you" (I Peter 5:2). Jesus told Peter: "Feed my lambs. . . . Feed my sheep. . . . Feed my sheep" (John 21:15-17). Of course, the food is the Word of God, which a preacher should give to his flock.

B. Lead them. "Neither as being lords over God's heritage, but being ensamples to the flock" (I Peter 5:3).

A preacher should lead his flock:

   in his example before them.
   in his love for the Lord.
   in his love for other Christians.
   in his love for the lost.
   in his everyday life.

C. Love them. A preacher should love his people. Paul loved the Christians at Corinth and wrote to them of his love. ". . . Ye are in our hearts to die and live with you" (II Cor. 7:3). He wrote to the Thessalonians:"So being affectionately desirous of you, we were willing tc have imparted unto you, not the gospel of God only, but also our own souls, because ye were dear unto us" (I Thess. 2:8).

The reward to the preacher who takes heed to himself and to the doctrine is: "In doing this thou shalt both save thyself, and them that hear thee" (I Tim. 4:16). This means that he will save himself and others from wrong beliefs and wrong living.

The reward to the preacher who takes heed to the flock is: "And when the chief Shepherd shall appear, ye shall receive a crown of glory that fadeth not away" (I Peter 5:4).

May the Lord help you as a preacher to take heed unto yourself, unto the doctrine, and unto all the flock. "Remember you are God's sword, His instrument—I trust, a chosen vessel unto Him to bear His name."

2

DAILY DOZEN

Some years ago it was popular to speak of doing physical exercises. They were spoken of as the "daily dozen." The Bible speaks of doing spiritual exercises daily. I want to share with you twelve things God tells us to do daily.

I. **Praise God daily.**

Psalm 72:15 says: ". . . *daily** shall he be praised." We should praise God daily because of His benefits. David praised God when he said: "Blessed be the Lord, who *daily* loadeth us with benefits, even the God of our salvation" (Ps. 68:19). Paul praised God and exhorted others: "Rejoice in the Lord alway: and again I say, Rejoice" (Phil. 4:4).

II. **Pray daily.**

The Bible teaches that Christians should pray daily. The psalmist said: "Be merciful unto me, O Lord: for I cry unto thee *daily*" (Ps. 86:3). "Lord, I have called *daily* upon thee" (Ps. 88:9). The New Testament teaches us to "pray without ceasing" (I Thess. 5:17). "Praying always with all prayer and supplication in the Spirit, and watching thereunto with all perseverance and supplication for all saints" (Eph. 6:18).

III. **Search the Scriptures daily.**

It was said of the Christians in Berea that they "searched the scriptures *daily*, whether those things were so" (Acts 17:11). Psalm

---

*Italics mine here and throughout this volume when italic type appears within quotations from Scripture.

1 speaks of the blessed man. "His delight is in the law of the Lord; and in his law doth he meditate *day* and *night*. And he shall be like a tree planted by the rivers of water, that bringeth forth his fruit in his season; his leaf also shall not wither; and whatsoever he doeth shall prosper" (Ps. 1:2-3). The only place the word *success* is mentioned in the Bible is in Joshua 1:8, where success is promised to the person who meditates on the Word of God day and night, and obeys it.

IV. Watch daily.

"Blessed is the man that heareth me, watching *daily* at my gates, waiting at the posts of my doors" (Prov. 8:34). This implies an earnest, diligent, patient, hungering of the heart for the Lord and for all He has for us. Various interpretations have been given for "watching daily" and "waiting": an eager student watching and waiting for his teacher's appearance; clients crowding around a great man's door; Levites guarding the doors of the temple; a lover staying at the gate of his beloved so as not to miss her.

V. Fellowship daily.

It was said of the early Christians: "And they, continuing *daily* with one accord in the temple, and breaking bread from house to house, did eat their meat with gladness and singleness of heart" (Acts 2:46). "And they continued stedfastly in the apostles' doctrine and fellowship, and in breaking of bread, and in prayers" (Acts 2:42).

VI. Witness daily.

Every Christian should witness for the Lord daily. "And *daily* in the temple, and in every house, they ceased not to teach and preach Jesus Christ." This speaks of:

Daily evangelism—"daily."
Church evangelism—"in the temple."
House-to-house evangelism—"and in every house."
Every-Christian evangelism—"they."
Continuous evangelism—"ceased not."
Teaching evangelism—"to teach."
Preaching evangelism—"and preach."
Christ-centered evangelism—"Jesus Christ."

Those first-century Christians continued *"daily* with one accord in the temple" (Acts 2:46); witnessed *"daily"* (Acts 5:42); "and the Lord added to the church *daily* such as should be saved" (Acts 2:47).

VII. Reason daily.

Paul disputed (reasoned) "in the synagogue with the Jews, and with the devout persons, and in the market *daily* with them that met with him" (Acts 17:17), and "he departed from them, and separated the disciples, disputing [reasoning] *daily* in the school of one Tyrannus" (Acts 19:9). He wanted people to know the truth and be saved. This should be our desire also.

VIII. Exhort daily.

We are instructed in Hebrews 3:13. "But exhort one another *daily,* while it is called To day. . . ." This means to encourage one another. Surely there is a great need for this today because there are so many discouragements in life.

IX. Take up the cross daily.

Jesus Christ said: "If any man will come after me [determination], let him deny himself [denial], and take up his cross *daily* [death], and follow me" (Luke 9:23). Taking up the cross means death to self. Christians are commanded. "Likewise reckon ye also yourselves to be dead indeed unto sin, but alive unto God through Jesus Christ our Lord" (Rom. 6:11). This is to be daily and moment by moment.

X. Die daily.

Paul says: ". . . I die *daily*" (I Cor. 15:31). This means that he was daily exposed to death for Christ's sake. He said he stood in jeopardy every hour (I Cor. 15:30). He said in Romans 8:36: "For thy sake we are killed all the day long; we are accounted as sheep for the slaughter." He was confident that nothing or no one could separate a true child of God from the love of God in Christ Jesus our Lord (Rom. 8:35, 37-39). We, too, should be willing to be exposed to death daily for Christ's sake, knowing that we have God's protection and care.

XI. Care for churches daily.

Paul was daily concerned for all the churches. After speaking of the many sufferings he went through as he served the Lord (II Cor. 11:23-27), he concluded: "Besides those things that are without, that which cometh upon me *daily,* the care of all the churches" (II Cor. 11:28). He loved the Christians in the churches and wanted the very best for them.

God's desire for the churches today is given in I Cor. 12:25: "That there should be no schism in the body; but that the members should have the same care one for another."

XII. Perform vows daily.

David said to God: "So will I sing praise unto thy name for ever, that I may *daily* perform my vows" (Ps. 61:8). In Psalm 116 we read of six vows David made to God. He said he would:

"love the Lord" (v. 1).
"call upon" the Lord (vv. 2, 17).
"walk before the Lord" (v. 9).
"take the cup of salvation" (v. 13).
"pay my vows" in public (vv. 14, 18).
"offer . . . the sacrifice of thanksgiving" (v. 17a).

In the same Psalm he gives thirteen reasons for making these vows. God had:

"heard my voice" (v. 1).
heard "my supplication" (v. 1).
"inclined his ear unto me" (v. 2).
been "gracious" (v. 5).
been "righteous" (v. 5).
been "merciful" (v. 5).
preserved " the simple" (v. 6).
"helped me" (v. 6).
"dealt bountifully" with him (v. 7).
"delivered my soul from death" (v. 8).
"delivered my feet from falling" (v. 8).
given him many "benefits" (v. 12).
"loosed my bonds" (v. 16).

God's Word says concerning vows: "When thou vowest a vow unto God, defer not to pay it; for he hath no pleasure in fools: pay that which thou hast vowed. Better is it that thou shouldest not vow, than that thou shouldest vow and not pay" (Eccles. 5:4-5).

May God help you to practice this "daily dozen" and "exercise thyself rather unto godliness" (I Tim. 4:7).

3

DEAD MEN DO TELL TALES

Luke 16:19-31

Roger Touhy, a former member of Al Capone's gang, was shot down in front of his sister's home in Chicago in December, 1969. The police explained why he was killed in these words: "Touhy knew too much. The underworld was afraid of him and dead men don't talk." But they were mistaken—dead men do talk. God speaks of Abel after his death: ". . . he being dead yet speaketh" (Heb. 11:4). In our Bible passage above, Jesus gives us a picture of life's other side, a true story of what happens to men after they die. He tells especially of two men, Lazarus and the rich man, and as He does, these two men, though dead, still speak to us. Here is what they say.

I. **There is a Hell (v. 23a).**

After the rich man died and was buried, immediately we read: "And in hell he lift up his eyes. . . ." This tells us that as soon as an unsaved person dies he goes to Hell. The word *hell* is mentioned fifty-four times in the Bible. "The wicked shall be turned into hell, and all the nations that forget God" (Ps. 9:17).

II. **People who go there can see (v. 23b).**

"He lift up his eyes . . . and seeth Abraham afar off, and Lazarus in his bosom."

III. **People who go there are in torment (vv. 23-25, 28).**

Four times in this passage God speaks of torment.

"Being in torments" (v. 23).
"I am tormented in this flame" (v. 24).
"Thou art tormented" (v. 25).
"This place of torment" (v. 26).

IV. **People who go there can speak (v. 24).**
"And he cried and said. . . ."

V. **People who go there want mercy (v. 24).**
". . . Father Abraham, have mercy on me. . . ."
God offers mercy in this life, but it's too late for the sinner in the next life.

VI. **People who go there remember (v. 25).**
"But Abraham said, Son, remember. . . ."
Three times in Mark, Jesus speaks of people who go to Hell and says: "Where their worm dieth not. . . ." (Mark 9:44, 46, 48). Some commentators explain this to mean that the consciences of those in Hell will always trouble them and they will remember forever.

VII. **People who go there can't have visitors (v. 26).**
". . . They which would pass from hence to you cannot. . . ."
There is a great gulf fixed between the lost and the saved in eternity.

VIII. **People who go there can't get out (v. 26).**
Abraham, a saved man, said to the rich man in Hell, ". . . Neither can they pass to us, that would come from thence." The lost are in Hell forever.

IX. **People who go there do not want their loved ones to go to Hell (vv. 27-28).**
The man in Hell wanted someone to go and testify to his five brothers so that they wouldn't go to Hell. Nobody in Hell wants their loved ones to join them.

X. **People go there because they will not repent (v. 30).**
The rich man in Hell realized that if his brothers would repent they would not go to Hell (v. 30). He knew he was lost and in Hell because he had not repented.

XI. **Unsaved people living today would not repent if someone came back from the dead (v. 31).**
Abraham said to the rich man, "If they hear not Moses and the prophets [obey not the Word of God], neither will they be persuaded, though one rose from the dead."

XII. **People who are saved are comforted and in a much better place when they die (v. 25).**
I have been speaking about the tales a dead man in Hell tells us. Now

I want to tell you one more wonderful tale, or truth, which Lazarus, the saved man, tells us.

Lazarus died a saved man and had been "carried by the angels into Abraham's bosom" (v. 22). Abraham says of Lazarus: "Now he is comforted."

When a saved person dies, he immediately goes to be with the Lord (Phil. 1:21, 23; II Cor. 5:1-8), and is comforted by the Lord.

One day you will die. What tale will you tell after you are dead? Will it be what the rich man told, or will it be what Lazarus told? There is quite a difference.

Because Jesus died for our sins and rose again for our justification, we can be saved from our sins by repenting (Luke 13:3) and believing on the Lord Jesus Christ (Acts 16:31). Then, ". . . being now justified by his blood, we shall be saved from wrath through him" (Rom. 5:9). If you will open your heart to Jesus Christ, He will save you and open Heaven to you.

4

DON'T BE DECEIVED

Galatians 6:7

There are many things that will deceive you if you are not careful:
"the Devil" (Rev. 12:9).
"men" (II Tim. 3:13; Eph. 5:6).
the "heart" (Isa. 44:20; Jer. 17:9).
"sin" (Heb. 3:13).
"false prophets" (Matt. 24:11).
"false Christs" (Matt. 24:24).
"riches" (Matt. 13:22).
"wine" and "strong drink" (Prov. 20:1).
"pride" (Obad. 1:3).

Many times in the Bible God warns us about being deceived. A psychologist said, "The hardest person to help is the one who will not be honest with himself, the one who deceives himself."

I. Don't be deceived by saying you have no sin.

A person who says he has no sin is deceiving himself. "If we say we have no sin, we *deceive ourselves,* and the truth is not in us" (I John 1:8). The Bible makes it very plain that "all have sinned, and come short of the glory of God" (Rom. 3:23). "All we like sheep have gone astray; we have turned every one to his own way. . . ." (Isa. 53:6). "But we are all as an unclean thing, and all our righteousnesses are as filthy rags; and we do all fade as a leaf. . . ." (Isa. 64:6). "For there is not a just man upon earth, that doeth good, and sinneth not" (Eccles. 7:20). "They are all gone aside, they are all together become filthy: there is none that doeth good, no, not one"

(Ps. 14:3). "For I know that in me [that is, in my flesh] dwelleth no good thing. . . ." (Rom. 7:18).

II. Don't be deceived by thinking you are something.

"For if a man think himself to be something, when he is nothing, *he deceiveth himself*" (Gal. 6:3). There is no reason for any of us to be proud of ourselves and think we are really something because God says: ". . . Verily every man at his best state is altogether vanity" (Ps. 39:5). God speaks of the insignificance of man in Isaiah 40 and compares man and nations to:

"grass" (vv. 6-7).
"a drop of a bucket" (v. 15).
"the small dust of the balance" (v. 15).
"nothing" (v. 17).
"less than nothing" (v. 17).
"vanity" (v. 17).
"grasshoppers" (v. 22).

Paul asked the question: "For who maketh thee to differ from another? and what has thou that thou didst not receive? now if thou didst receive it, why dost thou glory, as if thou hadst not received it?" (I Cor. 4:7).

III. Don't be deceived by an unbridled tongue.

James says: "If any man among you seem to be religious, and bridleth not his tongue, but *deceiveth his own heart*, this man's religion is vain" (James 1:26). David gives very good advice concerning the tongue. "I said, I will take heed to my ways, that I sin not with my tongue: I will keep my mouth with a bridle, while the wicked is before me" (Ps. 39:1).

IV. Don't be deceived by wrong companions.

Paul warned: "*Be not deceived:* evil communications corrupt good manners" (I Cor. 15:33). This has been rendered: "Bad company ruins good morals." It *does* matter who our companions are. It has been said: "If you run with a skunk, you will smell like a skunk." This should be our testimony: "I am a companion of all them that fear thee, and of them that keep thy precepts" (Ps. 119:63).

V. Don't be deceived by being disobedient.

We are exhorted in James 1:22: "But be ye doers of the word, and not hearers only, *deceiving your own selves.*" A person who hears the Word of God, but does not obey it, is deceiving himself. One test for determining whether we really know God is given in I John

2:3-5. "And hereby we do know that we know him, if we keep his commandments. He that saith, I know him, and keepeth not his commandments, is a liar, and the truth is not in him. But whoso keepeth his word, in him verily is the love of God perfected: hereby know we that we are in him." Speaking of Christ, the writer of the Book of Hebrews said: "And being made perfect, he became the author of eternal salvation unto all them that obey him" (Heb. 5:9).

VI. Don't be deceived by thinking you will get by with sin.

An eternal truth is given in Galatians 6:7. "*Be not deceived;* God is not mocked: for whatsoever a man soweth, that shall he also reap." Nobody ever gets by with sin—sin will always be found out and punished. Moses told the people of Israel: ". . . Be sure your sin will find you out" (Num. 32:23). James said: ". . . Sin, when it is finished, bringeth forth death" (James 1:15).

VII. Don't be deceived by thinking you can practice sin and go to Heaven.

Paul speaks of this in Ephesians 5:5-6. "For this ye know, that no whoremonger, nor unclean person, nor covetous man, who is an idolator, hath any inheritance in the kingdom of Christ and of God. *Let no man deceive you* with vain words: for because of these things cometh the wrath of God upon the children of disobedience." He says something similar to this in I Corinthians 6:9-10. "Know ye not that the unrighteous shall not inherit the kingdom of God? *Be not deceived;* neither fornicators, nor idolaters, nor adulterers, nor effeminate, nor abusers of themselves with mankind, nor thieves, nor covetous, nor drunkards, nor revilers, nor extortioners, shall inherit the kingdom of God." Those who practice sin, continue in it, and refuse to turn from it, cannot go to Heaven.

Thank God, all of those mentioned above can be saved if they will repent of their sins and believe on the Lord Jesus Christ. God says: "And such were some of you: but ye are washed, but ye are sanctified, but ye are justified in the name of the Lord Jesus, and by the Spirit of our God" (I Cor. 6:11).

Don't be deceived—be delivered from sin and go to Heaven through our Lord Jesus Christ.

5

GOD'S LAST MESSAGE

Revelation 22:17-21

As God closes His Word to man in the Bible, He gives us His last message. Here we find the last invitation, the last warning, the last promise, and the last prayer in the Bible.

I. **The last invitation in the Bible (v. 17).**

"And the Spirit and the bride say, Come. And let him that heareth say, Come. And let him that is athirst come. And whosoever will, let him take the water of life freely."

This is one of the sweetest invitations in the Bible. Referring to this verse, D. L. Moody said that what must have happened was that God said to John, just before He closed this last book of the Bible, "John, in case people miss all of the other invitations in the Bible, write this last one."

A. The Spirit says, "Come." The Holy Spirit calls people to Christ (John 16:7-11).

B. The bride says, "Come." The *bride* refers to the true church (Eph. 5:25-32), and she calls people to Christ.

C. Those who hear say, "Come." Everyone who hears the message of Christ should call others to Christ.

D. The thirsty can come. Jesus said, "If any man thirst, let him come unto me, and drink" (John 7:37).

E. Whosoever will can come. The person who is willing to receive Jesus Christ as personal Saviour and Lord will be received by Jesus Christ. He promises, ". . . Him that cometh to me I will in no wise cast out" (John 6:37).

W. A. Criswell comments: "Oh, what a simple Gospel and what a simple message! Let him *take*. Does a man desire Christ? Let him *take* Christ. Does a man desire life? Let him *take* life. Does a man desire heaven? Let him *take* heaven. Does a man desire reconciliation? Let him *take* reconciliation. Does a man desire forgiveness? Let him *take* forgiveness. Does a man desire Jesus? Let him *take* the blessed Lord Jesus."

The little girl who gave a talk in Sunday school understood this. She said:"I'm going to give a talk on the word *come*. The letter *c* stands for children. Children are invited to come to Jesus, and if they come, Jesus will save them. The letter *o* stands for old people. Old people are invited to come to Jesus, and if they come, Jesus will save them. The letter *m* stands for middle-aged people. Middle-aged people are invited to come to Jesus, and if they come, Jesus will save them. The letter *e* stands for everybody. Everybody is invited to come to Jesus, and Jesus promises to save everybody who comes to Him."

If you have never responded to this last invitation, come to Him now and receive Christ as your own Saviour and Lord. Say with the songwriter:

> Just as I am, without one plea,
> But that thy blood was shed for me,
> And that thou bidd'st me come to Thee,
> O Lamb of God, I come! I come!

Charlotte Elliott

II. The last warning in the Bible (vv. 18-19).

This is a warning about adding to the things written in this Book of Revelation (v. 18), or taking away from the things written in this book (v. 19). God not only warns about adding or taking from this book, His warnings pertain to the whole Bible. Close to the beginning of the Bible (Deut. 4:2), near the middle of the Bible (Prov. 30:6), and here at the close (Rev. 22:18-19), God solemnly warns about the awful judgments that will come upon those who add to or take away from His Word. Those who do so have no part in the book of life. A true Christian will not tamper with the Word of God, only lost critics, who are arrogant and unbelieving, dare such a thing.

III. The last promise in the Bible (v. 20a).

Jesus gave the last promise in the Bible: "Surely I come quickly." Three times in this last chapter of the Bible He promises He will come quickly (vv. 7, 12, 20). His coming is elsewhere described as:

"nigh" (James 5:8).
"at the doors" (Matt. 24:33).
"lightning" (Luke 17:24).
"a snare" (Luke 21:35).
"yet a little while" (Heb. 10:37)
"in a moment" (I Cor. 15:52).
"suddenly" (Mark 13:36).

When He comes again to take His own, He will come quickly, without a moment's notice; and all who are His will be changed in a moment, but all who are not His will be left. There are many indications that His coming is near, and if you are not ready, He warns, "Therefore be ye also ready, for in such an hour as ye think not the Son of man cometh" (Matt. 24:44). The way to be ready is to be saved, and the way to be saved is to repent of your sins (Luke 13:3) and believe on the Lord Jesus Christ (Acts 16:31).

IV. **The last prayer in the Bible (v. 20b).**

After Jesus promised He would come quickly, John prayed, "Even so, come, Lord Jesus." John wanted Jesus to come. The coming of Jesus is:

a comforting hope (I Thess. 4:16-18).
"a blessed hope" (Titus 2:13).
a purifying hope (I John 3:3).

Paul said that those who loved the appearing of Jesus Christ would receive a crown of righteousness when He comes (II Tim. 4:8).

William R. Newell, in *The Book of the Revelation,* states:"No unwillingness to have God's will done on earth as in heaven possessed the heart of the apostle; no plans of his own, however earnest, held back the eager call of his heart to the Lord to come; no concern for those yet unsaved who might be near and dear, or for whom his soul was burdened, could for an instant invade the inner sanctuary of his soul where *he awaited his Lord from heaven!* And so should it be with us! "

The last prayer in the Bible should be the first prayer on the lips of every Christian.

My prayer is that you may be ready for His coming, looking for His coming, waiting for His coming, working for His coming, loving His coming, desiring His coming, and praying for His coming.

6

HERE'S HELP

Psalm 12

Recently, the following letter from a teenager appeared in *The Christian Reader:*

Dear Christian Reader,

I'm a thirteen-year-old girl. I go to a very nice, well-mannered church. We have a wonderful pastor, but what our church needs is an old-fashioned revival!

Our pastor once spoke on starting a revival, and he said it would have to begin with the young people. I'd like to know, though, how we're going to get started. We need a person or persons who will step out and help us spiritually.

For example, adults at our church think that our dresses are too short, we wear too much make-up, or we don't behave well. I admit that some of this is true, but I also say that if the adults would help us, instead of criticizing, a revival could be possible.

Teens nowadays are looking for a way to get in touch with God, but they are not getting help from adults. Not all adults are this way, but there are quite a few of them. We need someone to show us the right path and we're crying for a way to get in touch with Jesus.

I'm a missionary's kid, and I am writing like this because I know how the teens feel. I wish more than anything that you would publish this because maybe somebody will understand and try to help us. Thank you.

Three times this girl pleaded for someone to "help us." She wanted help to "get in touch with God," "to get in touch with Jesus," and help so that a "revival could be possible." Millions of people in this country and in the world are crying for someone to "help us." In this message I want to help you. When a person is out of touch with God and Jesus, it's either because the person is unsaved or backslidden. The person who is unsaved needs to be regenerated, and the backslidden person needs to be restored to fellowship with God.

I. Here's help to be regenerated.

If you are unsaved, you are out of touch with God, separated from God, and cannot get in touch with Him until you are regenerated, or born again. Jesus said: "Ye must be born again" (John 3:7). In order to be born again you must receive Jesus Christ as your personal Saviour. When you receive Him as your personal Saviour and Lord, he gives you "power to become the sons [children] of God, even to them that believe on his name" (John 1:12). You become His child, "born . . . of God" (John 1:13), no longer separated, but "made nigh by the blood of Christ" (Eph. 2:13).

Thank God, you can be regenerated today.

II. Here's help to be restored.

When a Christian sins, he gets out of touch with God and needs to be restored to fellowship with Him. Here's help from God's Word:

"If we confess our sins, he is faithful and just to forgive us our sins, and to cleanse us from all unrighteousness" (I John 1:9).

"He that covereth his sins shall not prosper: but whoso confesseth and forsaketh them shall have mercy" (Prov. 28:13).

"Return, thou backsliding Israel, saith the Lord; and I will not cause mine anger to fall upon you: for I am merciful, saith the Lord, and I will not keep anger for ever. Only acknowledge thine iniquity, that thou hast transgressed against the Lord thy God . . . and ye have not obeyed my voice, saith the Lord. Turn, O backsliding children, saith the Lord; for I am married unto you. . . . Return, ye backsliding children, and I will heal your backslidings. . . ." (Jer. 3:12-14, 22). Backslidden Christian, God offers you help. He promises that if you will confess and forsake your sins and return to Him, He will restore you to fellowship with Himself. Thank God, you can be restored today.

III. Here's help to be revived.

The young girl said if the adults "would help us instead of criticizing, a revival could be possible." Here's help to be revived. Charles G. Finney, the well-known revivalist, gives some helpful words on revival.

A revival is the renewal of the first love of Christians, resulting in the awakening and conversion of sinners to God. It consists in the return of a church from her backslidings, and in the conversion of sinners.

1. It always includes conviction of sin on the part of the church.
2. Backslidden Christians will be brought to repentance.
3. Christians will have their faith renewed.
4. A revival breaks the power of the world and of sin over Christians.
5. When the churches are thus awakened and reformed, the salvation of sinners will follow.

Christians are to be blamed more for not being revived than sinners are to be blamed for not being converted.

R. A. Torrey, world-famous evangelist, gave a prescription for a revival.

A. Let a few Christians (they need not be many) get thoroughly right with God themselves. This is the prime essential! If this is not done, the rest I am going to say will come to nothing.
B. Let them bind themselves together to pray for a revival until God opens the heavens and comes down.
C. Let them put themselves at the disposal of God, for Him to use as He sees fit in winning others to Christ. That is all.

This is sure to bring a revival to any church or community. I have personally given this prescription around the world. It has been taken by many communities, and in no instance has it ever failed; and it cannot fail!

Someone else has written:

> If all the sleeping folk will *wake up,*
> And all the lukewarm folk will *fire up,*
> And all the dishonest will *confess up,*
> And all the disgruntled folk will *sweeten up,*
> And all the discouraged folk will *cheer up,*
> And all the depressed folk will *look up,*
> And all the estranged folk will *make up,*
> And all the gossipers will *shut up,*
> And all the dry bones will *shake up,*
> And all the true soldiers will *stand up,*
> And all the Church Members will *pray up*
> Then—*you can have a revival!*

God Himself has given a prescription for revival:

> If my people, which are called by my name
> > shall humble themselves,
> > and pray,
> > and seek my face,
> > and turn from their wicked ways,

> then will I

> > hear from heaven,
> > and will forgive their sin,
> > and will heal their land.

II Chronicles 7:14.

Thank God, you can be revived today. Pray this threefold prayer concerning revival:

"revive *us*" (Ps. 85:6).
"revive *thy work*" (Hab. 3:2).
"revive *me*" (Ps. 138:7).

In Psalm 12:1 David cried, "Help, Lord. . . ." In verse 5 God promises help. God will also give you the help you need. He says to you: "Here's help."

You can be regenerated, you can be restored, you can be revived. Take God's help, which He offers today.

7

HOW CAN I FIND
GOD'S WILL FOR MY LIFE?

Romans 12:1-2

A few years ago, a poll was taken by the pastor of a large church in America to determine the topics people wanted their pastor to address from the pulpit. Over 5,000 people responded and the computer came up with ten topics which people most wanted to hear about. Second on the list, topped only by "Where Are We in Prophecy?" was the subject: "How Can I Find God's Will for My Life?" I want to discuss this topic with you.

I have written in the flyleaf of my Bible several sayings concerning the will of God:

> The secret of an unsatisfied life lies in an unsurrendered will.
>
> *Hudson Taylor*

> Inside the will of God there is no failure;
> outside the will of God there is no success.
> What is the end of life?
> The end of life is not to do good,
> although many of us think so.
> It is not to win souls,
> although I once thought so.
> The end of life is to do the will of God.
>
> *Henry Drummond*

> To *know* the will of God is the greatest knowledge,
> to *find* the will of God is the greatest discovery, and
> to *do* the will of God is the greatest achievement.
>
> *George Truett*

Romans 12:1-2, the text for this lesson, ends with "that good, and acceptable, and perfect, will of God." Preceding these words are four things which are necessary in order to discover God's will.

I. **You must be saved.**

"I beseech you therefore, *brethren....*"

God is speaking to those He calls "brethren." He is referring to those who are saved. God's will is for God's children. You will never find God's will for your life until you are saved. If you are not saved, God's will for you is that you be saved. Jesus said: "And this is the will of him that sent me, that every one which seeth the Son, and believeth on him, may have everlasting life: and I will raise him up at the last day" (John 6:40).

I Timothy 2:3-4 tells us that God desires all men to be saved. "For this is good and acceptable in the sight of God our Saviour; Who will have all men to be saved, and to come unto the knowledge of the truth." Peter says: "The Lord is ... not willing that any should perish, but that all should come to repentance" (II Peter 3:9).

If you have never repented (Luke 13:3) and believed on the Lord Jesus Christ (Acts 16:31), do this today, and then you will be able to find God's will.

II. **You must be surrendered.**

The rest of Romans 12:1 reads: "by the mercies of God, that ye present your bodies a living sacrifice, holy, acceptable unto God, which is your reasonable service." To find God's will for your life, God says you must be surrendered—you must "present your bodies a living sacrifice."

James H. McConkey wrote: "The supreme human condition of the fullness of the Spirit is a life wholly surrendered to God to do His will." Charles C. Ryrie provides the meaning of a surrendered life. "Simply stated, dedication concerns whether I will direct my life or whether Christ will."

The word *present* in v. 1 refers to a decisive step that a Christian takes once in his Christian life. This is made plain by the force of the Greek verb which is here translated "present." If an act is done again and again, the Greek uses the present tense. If an act is done only once in the past, the Greek uses the aorist tense. The word *present* here is in the aorist tense in the Greek, which means that this is an act done once and for all. As a sinner receives Christ as his Saviour only one time, so a Christian presents himself wholeheartedly to

God only once. The body represents the total person. When the Lord gets *you*, He will get your time, talent, money, and everything that belongs to you.

After the initial surrender comes the moment-by-moment and day-by-day submission and dependence on the Holy Spirit which is described by Paul. "Walk in the Spirit, and ye shall not fulfil the lust of the flesh" (Gal. 5:16).

You will never find God's will for your life until you are saved and surrendered to God.

III. You must be separated.

The third thing necessary in order to find God's will is set forth in the first part of Romans 12:2. "And be not conformed to this world." This has been rendered: "Don't let the world around you squeeze you into its own mold." The word *world* here should be translated "age," and does not refer to our planet and its mountains and plains, forests and fields, rivers and oceans. It is the world, or age, made up of godless and sinful human beings who think, act, and live apart from God.

Robert S. Candlish wrote: "The world is fallen humanity acting itself out in the human family." Samuel Rutherford said: "By the world is meant everything in it that is antagonistic to the Truth or to the life of God in the soul of men." God says: ". . . If any man love the world, the love of the Father is not in him" (I John 2:15). James states: ". . . know ye not that the friendship of the world is enmity with God? whosoever therefore will be a friend of the world is the enemy of God" (James 4:4). A Christian can fall prey to worldly temptation in his dress, speech, habits, expressions, mannerisms, styles, goals, ambitions, activities, standards, and programs. If the Christian allows these aspects of his life to be perverted by worldliness, he will never find God's will for his life.

G. Christian Weiss wrote in his excellent booklet *How To Know The Will of God:* "Quite frequently people come to me with the world literally painted all over their faces and ask me to pray that God may reveal His will to them. But God does not reveal His will to worldly Christians; they are not in a position to receive it. It is utterly vain for a person whose heart is in the world, whose life is patterned after the world, to ask prayer about knowing the will of God. God just does not reveal His will to such."

IV. You must be spiritually minded.

The next phrase in our text is, "but be ye transformed by the renewing of your mind." This refers to the adjustment of our moral and spiritual vision to the mind of God, and is accomplished by the Holy Spirit.

"But we all, with open face beholding as in a glass the glory of the Lord, are changed into the same image from glory to glory even as by the Spirit of the Lord" (II Cor. 3:18). The word *changed* here is a translation of the same Greek word which is rendered *transformed* in Romans 12:2—*metamorphoō*. It is the word from which our own word *metamorphosis* comes, and is also the same word used in Matthew 17:2 and Mark 9:2, describing the transfiguration of the Lord Jesus Christ.

To be transformed or transfigured into the image of Christ is the blessed privilege of the surrendered and separated Christian. We are transformed, "conformed to the image of his Son" (Rom. 8:29). "From the lowest of earth to the highest of Heaven," in the words of Norman B. Harrison. The "renewing of your mind" is done by the Holy Spirit. The entire self-life must come under His control.

Christians are commanded to "be filled with the Spirit" (Eph. 5:18). The Christian is instructed: "Grieve not the holy Spirit of God" (Eph. 4:30); "Quench not the Spirit" (I Thess. 5:19); and "Walk in the Spirit" (Gal. 5:16). If the Christian obeys the Word of God, then the Spirit of God will make him spiritually minded and show him the "good, and acceptable, and perfect, will of God" (Rom. 12:2).

It has been said that in the end there are only two kinds of people: those who have said to God, "Your will be done"; and those to whom God has said, "Your will be done."

Will you say to God, "Your will be done"? I pray that you will and that you will find the will of God, follow the will of God, and finish the will of God.

> Henceforth let my one ambition
> Be to know and do Thy will;
> All Thy loving heart desireth,
> In me, hour by hour, fulfill.
>
> "Good, acceptable, and perfect"
> They shall prove Thy will to be
> Who themselves have thus presented,
> Without one reserve, to Thee.

Katie F. Strickland

8

OPERATE IMMEDIATELY!

Mark 2:17

In our text Jesus says: "They that are whole have no need of the physician, but they that are sick. . . ." According to the Bible all of us are "sick"—spiritually sick.

No one is "clean" (Job 25:4).
No one is "good" (Ps. 14:3).
No one is "faithful" (Prov. 20:6).
No one is "pure" (Prov. 20:9).
No one is "just" (Eccles. 7:20).
No one is "better" than another (Rom. 3:9).
No one is "righteous" (Rom. 3:10).
No one "seeketh after God" (Rom. 3:11).
No one is profitable (Rom. 3:12).
No one is guiltless (Rom. 3:19).
No one is sinless (Rom. 3:23; Gal 3:22).

All of us need a physician—the Great Physician, the Lord Jesus Christ. He is the only one who can cure us from our spiritual sickness.

As we look into the Bible and see man's spiritual condition depicted there, we clearly see why we need the Great Physician to operate immediately in order to cure us and change us.

I. The patient's condition—the sinner from A to Z.
    A. Head.
       "Sick" (Isa. 1:5).
    B. Mind.
       "Wicked" (Prov. 21:27); proud (Dan. 5:20); "reprobate" (Rom. 1:28); "blinded" (II Cor. 4:4); vain (Eph. 4:17); "alienated"

(Col. 1:21); "puffed up" (Col. 2:18); "corrupt" (I Tim. 6:5); and "defiled" (Titus 1:15).

C. Eyes.

Fear not God (Ps. 36:1); "stand out with fatness" (Ps. 73:7); "never satisfied" (Prov. 27:20); "evil" (Prov. 28:22); "lofty" (Prov. 30:13); mocking (Prov. 30:17); covetous (Jer. 22:17); idolatrous (Ezek. 20:24); offending (Matt. 5:29); "full of adultery" (II Peter 2:14); and lustful (I John 2:16).

D. Ears.

Stopped (Ps. 58:4); "despise . . . wisdom" (Prov. 23:9); "uncircumcised" (Jer. 6:10); disobedient (Jer. 11:8); "dull of hearing" (Matt. 13:15); and "itching" (II Tim. 4:3).

E. Mouth.

"Full of cursing and deceit and fraud" (Ps. 10:7); "evil" (Ps. 50:19); sinful (Ps. 59:12); "speaketh vanity" (Ps. 144:8); "froward" (Prov. 4:24); "poureth out foolishness" (Prov. 15:2); "poureth out evil things" (Prov. 15:28); "devoureth iniquity" (Prov. 19:28); "flattering" (Prov. 26:28); boasting (Ezek. 35:13); and "full of cursing and bitterness" (Rom. 3:14).

F. Lips.

"Uncircumcised" (Exod. 6:12); "flattering" (Ps. 12:2); "lying" (Ps. 31:18); poisonous (Ps. 140:3); "perverse" (Prov. 4:24); transgressing (Prov. 12:13); contentious (Prov. 18:6); a "snare" (Prov. 18:7); "burning" (Prov. 26:23); and "unclean" (Isa. 6:5).

G. Tongue.

Flattering (Ps. 5:9); causing strife (Ps. 31:20); deceitful (Ps. 50:19); mischievous (Ps. 52:2); "a sharp sword" (Ps. 57:4); "false" (Ps. 120:3); "lying" (Prov. 12:19); "naughty" (Prov. 17:4); "perverse" (Prov. 17:20); "backbiting" (Prov. 25:23); "against the Lord" (Isa. 3:8); unbridled (James 1:26): "a fire, a world of iniquity" (James 3:6); untamed (James 3:8); and "an unruly evil, full of deadly poison" (James 3:8).

H. Face.

Painted (Jer. 4:30); "harder than a rock" (Jer. 5:3); and disfigured (Matt. 6:16).

I. Throat.

"An open sepulchre" (Rom. 3:13).

J. Neck.

Hardened (Prov. 29:1); "stretched forth" (Isa. 3:16); and "stiff" (Deut. 31:27; Jer. 17:23; Acts 7:51).

K. Thoughts.

"Evil continually" (Gen. 6:5); "vanity" (Ps. 94:11); and "iniquity" (Isa. 59:7).

L. Imaginations.

"Evil from his youth" (Gen. 8:21).

M. Conscience.

"Seared" (I Tim. 4:2); "defiled" (Titus 1:15); and "evil" (Heb. 10:22).

N. Understanding.

Lacking (Prov. 7:7); and "darkened" (Eph. 4:18).

O. Heart.

"Evil continually" (Gen. 6:5); "wicked" (Deut. 15:9); "double" (Ps. 12:2); mischievous (Ps. 28:3); erring (Ps. 95:10); of little worth (Prov. 10:20); foolish (Prov. 12:23); "proud" (Prov. 16:5); "haughty" (Prov. 18:12); "snares and nets" (Eccles. 7:26); "full of evil, and madness. . . ." (Eccles. 9:3); "revolting and . . . rebellious" (Jer. 5:23); "deceitful" (Jer. 17:9); covetous and violent (Jer. 22:17); stiff (Ezek. 2:4); "stony" (Ezek. 36:26); "set . . . on iniquity" (Hosea 4:8); "far" from God (Matt. 15:8); "uncircumcised" (Acts 7:51); "foolish . . . darkened" (Rom. 1:21); hard and impenitent (Rom. 2:5); and unbelieving (Heb. 3:12).

P. Hands.

"Mischief, . . . and full of bribes" (Ps. 26:10); violent (Ps. 58:2); "full of blood" (Isa. 1:15); doing "witchcraft" (Mic. 5:12); "do evil . . . earnestly" (Mic. 7:3); "unclean" (Hag. 2:14); and "wicked" (Acts 2:23).

Q. Feet.

"Run to evil" (Prov. 1:16); "swift in running to mischief" (Prov. 6:18); and "swift to shed blood" (Rom. 3:15).

R. Bones.

"Full of the sin of his youth" (Job 20:11).

S. Flesh.

Corrupt (Gen. 6:12); unprofitable (John 6:63); "cannot please God" (Rom. 8:8); and full of sinful works (Gal. 5:19-21).

T. Inward Parts.

Wickedness (Ps. 5:9).

U. Height.

Short of God's standard (Rom. 3:23).

V. Weight.

"Lighter than vanity" (Ps. 62:9); "found wanting" (Dan. 5:27).

W. Ways.

"Stubborn" (Judg. 2:19); "grievous" (Ps. 10:5); "folly" (Ps. 49:13); "lying" (Ps. 119:29); "darkness" (Prov. 2:13; 4:19); "crooked" (Prov. 2:15); lead to "death" (Prov. 14:12); "evil" (Prov. 28:10); "wicked" (Ezek. 13:22); "destruction and misery" (Rom. 3:16); and "unstable" (James 1:8).

X. State.

"Altogether vanity" (Ps. 39:5).

Y. Feelings.

"Past feeling" (Eph. 4:19).

Z. His Complete Condition.

". . . The whole head is sick, and the whole heart faint. From the sole of the foot even unto the head there is no soundness in it. . . ." (Isa. 1:5-6).

II. **The physician's cure.**

Jesus Christ, the Great Physician, is the only one who can cure the patient of his hopeless condition. As the sinner trusts the Saviour, all his sins are forgiven and he is made a new creature (II Cor. 5:17).

No case is "too hard" for the Great Physician (Jer. 32:17).

No case is "cast out," or refused, by the Great Physician (John 6:37).

No case is ever lost by the Great Physician (John 10:27-29).

No charge is ever assessed by the Great Physician (Rom. 6:23).

This physician is always available. Commit your case to Him today.

III. **The patient's change.**

When the Great Physician cures a person, that person is changed completely. "Therefore if any man be in Christ, he is a new creature: old things are passed away; behold, all things are become new" (II Cor. 5:17). Paul says of those who have been saved and changed by Jesus Christ: ". . . Ye have put off the old man with his deeds; And have put on the new man, which is renewed in knowledge after the image of him that created him" (Col. 3:9-10). Instead of his whole head being sick, his whole heart being faint, and having no soundness from the sole of the foot even unto the head (Isa. 1:5-6), the changed person is made "every whit whole" (John 7:23).

Jesus asked the man with an infirmity at the pool of Bethesda, "Wilt thou be made whole?" (John 5:6). When the man believed Jesus, "immediately the man was made whole" (John 5:9).

Right now, you can come to Jesus in all your need, wanting to be made whole, and trust Him as your personal Saviour and Lord, and He will cure you of all your spiritual sickness and change you completely. The Great Physician asks, "Wilt *thou* be made whole?" I pray that you will respond, "Operate immediately!"

> The Great Physician now is near,
> The sympathizing Jesus;
> He speaks the drooping heart to cheer,
> Oh, hear the voice of Jesus.
>
> Your many sins are all forgiv'n,
> Oh, hear the voice of Jesus;
> Go on your way in peace to heav'n,
> And wear a crown with Jesus.

William Hunter

9

SEVEN THINGS GOD HATES

Proverbs 6:16-19

It may seem strange to hear that God hates. People like to think of God as a God of love, and He is, but He is also a God who hates sin. In the Old Testament we read that God hated sin so much that He destroyed all of the human race He had created, all but eight people who believed Him and were preserved in the ark. "And God saw that the wickedness of man was great in the earth, and that every imagination of the thoughts of his heart was only evil continually. And it repented the Lord that he had made man on the earth, and it grieved him at his heart. And the Lord said, I will destroy man whom I have created from the face of the earth; both man, and beast, and the creeping thing, and the fowls of the air; for it repenteth me that I have made them"(Gen. 6:5-7).

God hates sin so much that He gave His only begotten Son, the Lord Jesus Christ, to pay for our sins so that we could be forgiven. "For Christ also hath once suffered for sins, the just for the unjust, that he might bring us to God. . . ." (I Peter 3:18).

Yes, God is a holy God and hates sin. Here are seven things He hates.

I. God hates "a proud look" (v. 17).

It was through pride that the devil fell. This was the first sin in the universe. Lucifer lifted himself up in pride and was cast out by God, and since then he has been the devil (Isa. 14:12-15; Ezek. 28:12-17). ". . . *Pride* and arrogancy, and the evil way, and the froward mouth, do I hate" (Prov. 8:13). Other verses in the Bible speak of pride. "*Pride* goeth before destruction, and an haughty spirit before a fall"

(Prov. 16:18). "A man's *pride* shall bring him low. . . ." (Prov. 29:23). "Behold, I am against thee, O thou most *proud*. . . ." (Jer. 50:31). ". . . Those that walk in *pride* he is able to abase" (Dan. 4:37). ". . . God resisteth the *proud*. . . ." (James 4:6).

II. God hates "a lying tongue" (v. 17).

"*Lying* lips are abomination to the Lord. . . ." (Prov. 12:22). Jesus said of the devil: ". . . He is a *liar,* and the father of it" (John 8:44). God's Word makes it plain that no liars shall enter the Holy City, New Jerusalem (Rev. 21:27). ". . . All *liars* shall have their part in the lake which burneth with fire and brimstone: which is the second death" (Rev. 21:8). Paul wrote in Ephesians 4:25: "Wherefore putting away *lying,* speak every man truth with his neighbor. . . ." We should pray with the psalmist: "Deliver my soul, O Lord, from *lying* lips, and from a deceitful tongue" (Ps. 120:2).

III. God hates "hands that shed innocent blood" (v. 17).

The sixth commandment says: "Thou shalt not kill" (Exod. 20:13). Cain shed innocent blood when he killed his brother Abel. ". . . And wherefore slew he him? Because his own works were evil, and his brother's righteous" (I John 3:12). Then God's Word makes the application for us today. "Whosoever hateth his brother is a murderer and ye know that no murderer hath eternal life abiding in him" (I John 3:15). Do you hate anyone? If you do, God says you are a murderer, and He hates murderers.

IV. God hates "an heart that deviseth wicked imaginations" (v. 18).

God judges us according to the evil of our hearts, for Jesus said: "Whosoever looketh on a woman to lust after her hath committed adultery with her already in his heart" (Matt. 5:28). "As he thinketh in his heart, so is he. . . ." (Prov. 23:7). "For from within, out of the heart of men, proceed evil thoughts, adulteries, fornications, murders, thefts, covetousness, wickedness, deceit, lasciviousness, an evil eye, blasphemy, pride, foolishness: all these evil things come from within, and defile the man" (Mark 7:21-23).

In describing an acquaintance, someone said: "That man is an inventor. He is always inventing some evil thing." God hates a heart that devises wicked things.

> Sow a thought and you reap a deed.
> Sow a deed and you reap a character.
> Sow a character and you reap a destiny.

V.   God hates "feet that be swift in running to mischief" (v. 18).

This speaks of evil actions. Evil imaginations lead to actual sins. Thomas à Kempis said: "Sin is first a simple suggestion, then a strong imagination, then desire, then delight, then assent." "Running to mischief" speaks not only of those who do mischief but also of those who are eager to do it. God hates this.

VI.   God hates "a false witness that speaketh lies" (v. 19).

The ninth commandment says: "Thou shalt not bear false witness against thy neighbour" (Exod. 20:16). God hates slander and has commanded: "Let no corrupt communication proceed out of your mouth. . . . Let all bitterness, and wrath, and anger, and clamour, and evil speaking, be put away from you, with all malice" (Eph. 4:29, 31). "These are the things that ye shall do; Speak ye every man the truth to his neighbour; execute the judgment of truth and peace in your gates: And let none of you imagine evil in your hearts against his neighbour; and love no false oath: for all these are things that I hate, saith the Lord" (Zech. 8:16-17).

VII.   God hates the person "that soweth discord among brethren" (v. 19).

God's Word speaks of the destructive nature of this. "An hypocrite with his mouth destroyeth his neighbour. . . ." (Prov. 11:9). "A froward man soweth strife: and a whisperer separateth chief friends" (Prov. 16:28). God wants unity among the brethren, not discord. "Behold, how good and how pleasant it is for brethren to dwell in unity!" (Ps. 133:1).

We should be very concerned that we are free from the seven sins above. If you are not saved, repent of your sins (all of them, not just these seven) and receive Jesus Christ as your personal Saviour and Lord (Luke 13:3; John 1:12). God will cleanse you from every sin (Acts 13:38-39; I John 1:7; Heb. 10:17), and will give you power to keep free from sin.

If you are a Christian and find some of these things in your life, confess your sins to God, and He has promised: "If we confess our sins, he is faithful and just to forgive us our sins, and to cleanse us from all unrighteousness" (I John 1:9). Then, rely on the Holy Spirit for victory. Let Him fill you (Eph. 5:18), and claim His promise: "Walk in the Spirit, and ye shall not fulfil the lust of the flesh" (Gal. 5:16).

10

SEVEN WAYS TO
LENGTHEN YOUR LIFE

Proverbs 10:27a

The Word of God teaches that a person can lengthen, or prolong, his life. "The fear of the Lord prolongeth days" (Prov. 10:27a). As I have studied the Bible I have found at least seven ways we can lengthen our lives.

I. **You can lengthen your life by obeying your parents.**

"Honor thy father and thy mother: that *thy days may be long upon the land* which the Lord thy God giveth thee" (Exod. 20:12). Ephesians 6:1-3 states almost the same thing. "Children, obey your parents in the Lord: for this is right. Honor thy father and mother; which is the first commandment with promise; that it may be well with thee, and *thou mayest live long on the earth.*"

II. **You can lengthen your life by praying and weeping.**

When told he was going to die, King Hezekiah "turned his face toward the wall, and prayed unto the Lord, and said, Remember now, O Lord, I beseech thee, for I have walked before thee in truth and with a perfect heart, and have done that which is good in thy sight. And Hezekiah wept sore. Then came the word of the Lord to Isaiah, saying, Go, and say to Hezekiah, Thus saith the Lord, the God of David thy father, I have heard thy prayer, I have seen thy tears: behold, *I will add unto thy days fifteen years*" (Isa. 38:2-5).

III. **You can lengthen your life by being honest.**

"But thou shalt have a perfect and just weight, a perfect and just measure [honesty] shalt thou have: that *thy days may be lengthened in the land* which the Lord thy God giveth thee" (Deut. 25:15).

IV. **You can lengthen your life by hating covetousness.**

". . . He that hateth covetousness shall *prolong his days*" (Prov. 28:16).

V. **You can lengthen your life by obeying God's Word.**

"Thou shalt keep therefore his statutes, and his commandments, which I command thee this day, that it may go well with thee, and with thy children after thee, and that *thou mayest prolong thy days upon the earth,* which the Lord thy God giveth thee, for ever" (Deut. 4:40). (See also Deut. 5:33; 6:2; 11:8-9; 32:45-47.)

"My son, forget not my law; but let thine heart keep my commandments: for *length of days, and long life, and peace, shall they add to thee*" (Prov. 3:1-2).

VI. **You can lengthen your life by putting to death the deeds of the body.**

This must be done by the power of the Spirit of God as He controls the life. ". . . If ye through the Spirit do mortify [put to death] the deeds of the body, *ye shall live*" (Rom. 8:13). "Walk in the Spirit, and ye shall not fulfil the lust of the flesh" (Gal. 5:16).

VII. **You can lengthen your life by trusting Jesus Christ as your personal Saviour.**

Our text says that "the fear of the Lord prolongeth days." To fear the Lord means to reverence and trust Him. As you trust the Lord Jesus Christ as your personal Saviour, He promises: "For God so loved the world, that he gave his only begotten Son, that whosoever believeth in him should not perish, but *have everlasting life*" (John 3:16). Thank God, we can *live forever* when Jesus Christ is our personal Saviour.

> When we've been there ten thousand years,
> Bright shining as the sun,
> We've no less days to sing God's praise
> Than when we first begun.

John Newton

11

SEVEN WAYS TO
SHORTEN YOUR LIFE

Proverbs 10:27

In our text we are told that as well as prolonging his life, a person can also shorten his life. "The years of the wicked shall be shortened." Throughout God's Word we are taught that a person can shorten his life because of sin. "Hast thou marked the old way which wicked men have trodden? Which were cut down out of time, whose foundation was overflown with a flood" (Job 22:15-16). *The Amplified Bible* renders verse 16, "men who were snatched away before their time."

". . . Bloody and deceitful men shall not live out half of their days. . . ." (Ps. 55:23). God asks: "Why shouldest thou die before thy time?" (Eccles. 7:17). Here are seven ways to shorten your life.

I. **You can shorten your life by disobedience.**

Adam and Eve disobeyed God and shortened their lives (Gen. 2:15-17; 3:6-7, 22-24). They would have lived forever if they had not sinned.

The people in Noah's day disobeyed God and shortened their lives (Gen. 6:5-7; 7:21-22).

Lot's wife disobeyed God and shortened her life (Gen. 19:15-17, 26).

Nadab and Abihu disobeyed God and shortened their lives (Lev. 10:1-2).

Moses disobeyed God and shortened his life (Num. 20:7-12; Deut. 3:25-27; 34:5-7).

The men who disobeyed God and looked into the ark shortened their lives (Num. 4:17-20: I Sam. 6:19).

Uzzah disobeyed God and shortened his life (II Sam. 6:6-7).

II. **You can shorten your life by dishonesty.**

"As the partridge sitteth on eggs, and hatcheth them not; so he that getteth riches, and *not by right, shall leave them in the midst of his days,* and at his end shall be a fool" (Jer. 17:11).

Achan brought death to himself and his family by dishonesty (Josh. 7:19-21, 24-26).

III. **You can shorten your life by rebellion.**

Korah shortened his life by rebellion (Num. 16:1-2, 31-33).

Hananiah shortened his life by rebellion (Jer. 28:15-17).

IV. **You can shorten your life by hardening your neck (stubbornness).**

"He, that being often reproved hardeneth his neck, shall suddenly be destroyed, and that without remedy" (Prov. 29:1). Stubbornness has shortened the lives of many people.

V. **You can shorten your life by lying to God.**

Ananias and Sapphira shortened their lives by lying to God (Acts 5:1-10).

VI. **You can shorten your life by living after the flesh.**

"For if ye live after the flesh, ye shall die. . . ." (Rom. 8:13). Living after the flesh means doing what the sinful old nature desires. This has shortened the lives of many people.

VII. **You can shorten your life by not judging yourself.**

"For if we would judge ourselves, we should not be judged. But when we are judged, we are chastened of the Lord, that we should not be condemned with the world" (I Cor. 11:31-32). When God chastens His children and they do not respond by judging themselves and confessing and forsaking their sins, He sometimes takes their lives prematurely. This is called "sin unto death," a physical death which shortens lives (I John 5:16).

Let me ask you the question in Ecclesiastes 7:17. "Why shouldest thou die before thy time?" Don't be disobedient, dishonest, rebellious, stubborn, full of lies, living after the flesh and failing to judge yourself. Put your trust completely in the Lord Jesus Christ and let Him make you obedient, honest, yielded, submissive, and truthful; one who lives after the Spirit and judges himself.

12

THE BIGGEST KILLER

Romans 6:23

There are many killers in this world, such as heart disease, cancer, alcohol, and smoking. The biggest killer of all, however, is sin.

I. **What is sin?**

    A. Lawlessness (I John 3:4).

    B. Selfishness. ". . . We have turned every one to his own way. . . ." (Isa. 53:6). "For men shall be lovers of their own selves. . . ." (II Tim. 3:2).

    C. The evil principle within. "Now if I do that I would not, it is no more I that do it, but sin that dwelleth in me" (Rom. 7:20).

    D. The thing God hates. "Oh, do not this abominable thing that I hate" (Jer. 44:4).

    E. Coming "short of the glory of God" (Rom. 3:23).

    F. The thought of foolishness. "The thought of foolishness is sin. . . ." (Prov. 24:9).

    G. "An high look, and a proud heart, and the plowing of the wicked" (Prov. 21:4).

    H. Despising your neighbour (Prov. 14:21).

    I. Having "respect to persons" (James 2:9).

    J. "Rebellion . . . and stubbornness" (I Sam 15:23).

    K. Disobedience (Jer. 3:25).

    L. Backsliding (Jer. 14:7).

    M. Unbelief (John 16:9).

N. Omission (James 4:17).

O. "Whatsoever is not of faith" (Rom. 14:23).

P. "All unrighteousness" (I John 5:17).

II. What are the effects of sin?

A. Causes all the tears, heartaches, suffering, disease, war, bloodshed, and death that have ever been or shall ever be.

B. Makes us all sinners (Rom. 5:12).

C. Keeps us from having "rest" and "peace" (Ps. 38:3; Isa. 57:20-21).

D. Deceives (Heb. 3:13).

E. Binds (Prov. 5:22).

F. Enslaves (John 8:34).

G. Brings "reproach" (Prov. 14:34).

H. Wrongs souls (Prov. 8:36).

I. Withholds "good things" (Jer. 5:25).

J. Separates us from God (Isa. 59:2).

K. Darkens "the understanding" (Eph. 4:18).

L. Sears the conscience (I Tim. 4:2).

M. Corrupts the "imagination" (Gen. 6:5).

N. Sends the soul to Hell forever (Matt. 25:46; Rom 6:23; Rev. 21:8.

O. Provokes God "to anger" (I Kings 16:2).

P. Sent Jesus Christ to the cross (Isa. 53:5-6; I Cor. 15:3; I Peter 2:24; 3:18).

III. What has God done about sin?

A. God sent His Son to die to pay the penalty for sin (John 3:16; Rom. 5:8; Rom 6:23a).

B. God sent His Son to put sin away (Isa. 53:6, 10-12; John 1:29; Heb. 9:26; I John 1:7; 3:5).

IV. What becomes of the sins of those who are saved?

God

A. Forgives them (Eph. 1:7; I John 2:12).

B. Removes them (Ps. 103:12).

C. Changes their color (Isa. 1:18).

D. Blots them out (Isa. 44:22).

E. Casts them behind His back (Isa. 38:17).

F. Casts them "into the depths of the sea" (Micah 7:19).

G. Forgets them (Isa. 43:25; Jer. 31:34; Heb. 8:12; 10:17).

V. What becomes of those who are not saved from their sins?

God will

A. "Recompense" (pay them back) (Jer. 16:18a). (See also Galatians 6:7.)

B. Judge (Rev. 20:11-15).

C. "Punish" (Isa. 13:11).

D. Pour out "indignation," "wrath," "tribulation," and "anguish" (Rom. 2:8-9). (See also John 3:36; Revelation 14:10, 11; 21:8.)

Yes, sin is the biggest killer, but thank God because "the gift of God is eternal life through Jesus Christ our Lord" (Rom. 6:23b). You can live forever if you fully trust Jesus Christ as your personal Lord and Saviour. He will give you eternal life, instead of death. Jesus promises: "And whosoever liveth and believeth in me shall never die" (John 11:26).

13

THE CHRISTIAN'S BODY

I Corinthians 6:13-20

The world is using the human body in publicity and advertising more than ever before. The body is exploited in magazines, newspapers, billboards, and television. Many people live under the mastery of bodily appetites and lusts, becoming slaves of their lower natures.

Sometimes Christians are guilty of thinking that their bodies are not important, rather their souls. The Bible says much concerning the Christian's body. It is very important that we see what God says about our bodies.

I. **The Christian's body is not for fornication.**

In our Scripture passage Paul mentions "the body" a number of times. He says in verse 13: "... Now the body is not for fornication. ..." *Fornication* means illegitimate sex among the unmarried; that is, premarital sex.

The Rockefeller, Carnegie, Mellon, Clark, and Hazen foundations paid Daniel Yankelovich, Inc. to conduct a survey among young people recently. The poll was a scientific sampling of the opinions of 3,522 youths between the ages of sixteen and twenty-five. 1,006 were in college, the remainder were working. Of those interviewed, 78% of the collegians and 66% of the noncollegians thought premarital sex was acceptable.

In New York, a pair of Johns Hopkins University sociologists report that today's teen-age couples have reversed the old tradition of getting married and then having a child. The sociologists said: "To marry and then to conceive is the exception among teenagers."

According to their studies, three-quarters of first pregnancies among teenagers are started before marriage, and only one-third of these pregnant teenagers will be married when the baby is born.

An article written by a fifteen-year-old girl appeared in the *Philadelphia Daily News* recently. The article had first appeared in her school newspaper. Included in the article was the statement: "Sex is a natural part of life and should be treated that way. With the knowledge of modern medicine, unwanted pregnancy will no longer have to be a problem and youth can enjoy premarital sex without fear."

God's Word teaches that fornication and adultery are sinful and His judgment is on those who indulge.

Flee fornication. Every sin that a man doeth is without the body; but he that committeth fornication sinneth against his own body (I Cor. 6:18).

For this is the will of God, even your sanctification, that ye should abstain from fornication (I Thess. 4:3).

Marriage is honourable in all, and the bed undefiled: but whoremongers and adulterers God will judge (Heb. 13:4).

Know ye not that the unrighteous shall not inherit the kingdom of God? Be not deceived: neither fornicators, nor idolators, nor adulterers, nor effeminate, nor abusers of themselves with mankind, nor thieves, nor covetous, nor drunkards, nor revilers, nor extortioners, shall inherit the kingdom of God (I Cor. 6:9-10).

II. The Christian's body is for the Lord.

In verse 13 we are instructed that "the body is . . . for the Lord." The Christian's body is not his own, "ye are not your own" (v. 19), but has been bought by the Lord, "for ye are bought with a price" (v. 20). The price paid is given in I Peter 1:18-19: "Forasmuch as ye know that ye were not redeemed with corruptible things, as silver and gold. . . . But with the precious blood of Christ. . . ."

A Christian is not his own because he has been:

A. Purchased by the Lord—"ye are bought with a price" (I Cor. 6:20).

B. Presented to the Lord—"thine they were, and thou gavest them me" (John 17:6).

C. Possessed by the Lord—"your body is the temple of the Holy Ghost" (I Cor. 6:19).

III. **The Christian's body is the temple of the Holy Spirit.**

Verse 19 says: "What? know ye not that your body is the temple of the Holy Ghost which is in you? . . ."

At the moment of salvation, Christ comes into a Christian, the Holy Spirit comes in, and God Himself comes in. "Jesus answered and said unto him, If a man love me, he will keep my words: and my Father will love him, and *we* will come unto him, and *make our abode with him*" (John 14:23). The most sacred thing on earth is the Christian's body.

IV. **The Christian's body is to glorify God.**

". . . Therefore glorify God in your body. . . ." We have been created for God's glory, "I have created him for my glory" (Isa. 43:7), and have been commanded: "Whether therefore ye eat, or drink, or whatsoever ye do, do all to the glory of God" (I Cor. 10:31).

Paul had an earnest desire to glorify God in his body. "According to my earnest expectation and my hope, that in nothing I shall be ashamed, but that with all boldness, as always, so now also Christ shall be magnified in my body, whether it be by life, or by death" (Phil. 1:20). He stated in II Cor. 4:10: "Always bearing about in the body the dying of the Lord Jesus, that the life also of Jesus might be made manifest in our body."

The first question in the Westminster Catechism is: "What is the chief end of man?" We are told: "The chief end of man is to glorify God, and to enjoy Him forever."

The way a Christian can glorify God is given to us by Jesus in John 15:8, "Herein is my Father glorified, that ye bear much fruit. . . ." In order to instruct us how to bear much fruit Jesus said: "I am the vine, ye are the branches: he that abideth in me, and I in him, the same bringeth forth much fruit. . . ." (John 15:5).

To abide in Christ we must obey Him. "If ye keep my commandments [obey], ye shall abide in my love. . . ." (John 15:10). To obey Him we must love Him. "If ye love me, keep my commandments" (John 14:15). Simply stated:

> If we really love Christ, we will obey Him;
> If we obey Him, we will abide in Him;
> If we abide in Him, we will bear much fruit;
> And if we bear much fruit, we shall glorify God.

Let us love Him, obey Him, abide in Him, and glorify God.

V. The Christian's body is to be controlled.

Paul said: "But I keep under my body, and bring it unto subjection; lest that by any means, when I have preached to others, I myself should be a castaway" (I Cor. 9:27). Paul did not let the appetites of his body control him and lead him into sin. He knew that if he did God would disapprove him and would not be able to use him in His service.

Paul also knew that the only way his body could be controlled was by permitting the Holy Spirit, who lived within, to control him. In Romans 8:13 he instructs Christians: "For if ye live after the flesh, ye shall die: but if ye through the Spirit do mortify [put to death] the deeds of the body, ye shall live."

A Christian is commanded: "And be not drunk with wine, wherein is excess; but be filled with the Spirit" (Eph. 5:18). We are instructed in Gal. 5:16: "Walk in the Spirit, and ye shall not fulfil the lust of the flesh."

VI. The Christian's body is to be presented to the Lord.

"I beseech you therefore, brethren, by the mercies of God, that ye present your bodies a living sacrifice, holy, acceptable unto God, which is your reasonable service" (Rom. 12:1). As Christians, we are to place our bodies at God's disposal for Him to use as He pleases. This is a significant presentation, in which we yield our bodies and the members of our bodies as instruments of righteousness to God (Rom. 6:13).

In the Bible we see that almost every part of our body has been affected by sin: the head, eyes, ears, mouth, lips, throat, heart, hands, and feet. When God saves us, He beseeches us to present our bodies and the members of our bodies to Him that He may use us to bring others to Christ. Christ's body became a bridge which spanned the gulf between God and man. Now He wants our bodies to become a bridge between Him and lost men.

King George V of England was addressing a world-wide audience by radio, when someone tripped on one of the many wires on the floor of the Columbia Broadcasting System studio. For a moment, the King's message went off the air. Seeing the problem, Harold Vivian, a radio engineer, spliced the broken wires by grasping the two ends and holding on for twenty minutes, until new wires could be connected. He literally "presented his body a living sacrifice" that the king's message might reach the world. God wants and needs our bodies to reach the whole world with King Jesus' message.

When a Christian presents his body to the Lord, realizing that his body is not for fornication but for the Lord, a temple of the Holy Spirit, then his body will be controlled and he will be able to glorify God.

In an advertising campaign a health spa uses the slogan "I want your body!" The Lord is saying to Christians: "Present your bodies." Have you given God your body? If not, will you do so now?

VII. The Christian's body is to be changed.

Salvation provides not only for life on this earth, but it also provides for life after death. "Behold, I shew you a mystery; we shall not all sleep [die], but we shall all be changed, in a moment, in the twinkling of an eye, at the last trump: for the trumpet shall sound, and the dead shall be raised incorruptible, and we shall be changed" (I Cor. 15:51-52).

God explains: "For our conversation [citizenship] is in heaven: from whence also we look for the Saviour, the Lord Jesus Christ: who shall change our vile body, that it may be fashioned like unto his glorious body. . . ." (Phil. 3:20-21).

The Christian's body will be changed from:

Corruption to incorruption (I Cor. 15:42).

Dishonour to glory (I Cor. 15:43a).

Weakness to power (I Cor. 15:43b).

Natural to spiritual (I Cor. 15:44).

Our present bodies to one like Christ's resurrected body (Phil. 3:20-21).

A solid, physical body (Luke 24:39).

Made up of flesh and bones (Luke 24:39).

Yet different than our present bodies (John 20:19).

Kenneth A. Wuest wrote concerning the Christian's body:

But the body the believer will have after death is a spiritual body. . . . The future physical body will be so adjusted that it will be the efficient organ of the spirit. . . . We will be occupied entirely with God and His worship and service. . . .

The future physical body will have no death in it, no weakness, deformity, disease. The parts that have been removed, will be restored. What a blessed state that will be, to have a body which can never die, in which there will be no indwelling sinful nature, which will never become weary or exhausted, in which there will never be any pain. . . .

Our future bodies will be made of flesh and bones, the same flesh and bones we have now, but changes as to composition. . . .

Our Lord in His physical body of flesh and bones went through the stone walls of the building in which the disciples were meeting. The doors of the room were closed. We will be capable of the same thing also.

Thus, in the life to come, believers will cover their bodies with an enswathement of glory, a light covering, which will be produced from within.

14

THE COMMITTED LIFE

Psalm 37:5

The Christian life is described in a number of ways in the Bible:

>abundant (John 10:10).
>"crucified" (Gal. 2:20).
>fruitful (John 15:5).
>overflowing (John 7:37-39).
>"separate" (II Cor. 6:17).
>"filled with the Spirit" (Eph. 5:18).
>"transformed" (Rom. 12:1-2).

It is also described in our text as committed life.

I.   **The act of committal—"commit thy way unto the Lord."**

    A. *Commit* means to hand over, give in charge to. Just as we commit our money to the bank, where it is safe, so we commit our lives to the Lord, where we are safe.

    B. "Thy way" refers to our whole life—spirit, soul, body, loved ones, home, health, possessions, job, plans, past, present, future, our all. This committal can be made in a moment. Romans 12:1 refers to this in the words: "present your bodies a living sacrifice." The Williams' translation uses the wording "make a decisive dedication."

    C. "Unto the Lord" indicates we are to hand over everything to the Lord. If you have never done this, then right now, commit your way definitely, finally, and irrevocably to God as His child.

II. **The attitude of committal—"trust also in him."**

A. We are not only to commit our way to God, but we are also to trust Him: we are not only to take our hands off our lives, but we must also let Him put His hands on as He sees fit.

B. James H. McConkey says it well. "The 'commit' that puts all *into* his hands needs the 'trust also' that keeps all things *under* His hand."

C. Where there is the committal *of* all things, there should also be submission *in* all things, and we should say with Paul: ". . . I know whom I have believed, and am persuaded that he is able to keep that which I have committed unto him against that day" (II Tim. 1:12).

III. **The accomplishment of committal—"he shall bring it to pass."**

A. God will accomplish all that is for His glory and all that is for the Christian's good in the life of a committed Christian.

B. He has promised: "And we know that all things work together for good to them that love God, to them who are the called according to his purpose" (Rom. 8:28).

C. When we commit our money to the bank, we receive interest or dividends. According to Psalm 37, when we commit our way to the Lord, we also receive interest or dividends.

1. "They shall inherit the earth" (v. 9). (See also vv. 11, 18, 22, 29, 34.)

2. "The meek . . . shall delight themselves in the abundance of peace" (v. 11).

3. "The Lord upholdeth the righteous" (v. 17).

4. "They are preserved forever" (v. 28).

5. "None of his steps shall slide" (v. 31).

6. "He is their strength in the time of trouble" (v. 39).

7. "And the Lord shall help them, and deliver them" (v. 40).

Is your life the committed life? If not, make the act of committal today and follow through with the attitude of committal. Then you will be assured that God will accomplish the committal of your life.

15

THE EYES OF THE LORD

Proverbs 5:21

On Mount Palomar in California there is a 500-ton telescope, with a 200-inch mirror on top of a spider-web tube as tall as a five-story building. Its range is over 7 sextillion miles and its cost is $6 million. In spite of this range, it does not compare with the eyes of the Lord.

I. **The eyes of the Lord see all people.**
    "Thou God seest *me*" (Gen. 16:13).
    "His eyes behold the *nations*" (Ps. 66:7).
    "Neither is there *any creature* that is not manifest in his sight: but *all things* are naked and opened unto the eyes of him with whom we have to do" (Heb. 4:13).

II. **The eyes of the Lord see all the ways of people.**
    "For the ways of man are before the eyes of the Lord, and he pondereth all his goings" (Prov. 5:21). (See also Job 31:4; 34:21; Jer. 16:17; 32:19.)

III. **The eyes of the Lord are in every place.**
    "The eyes of the Lord are in every place...." (Prov. 15:3).

IV. **The eyes of the Lord see all evil.**
    "The eyes of the Lord are in every place, beholding the evil...." (Prov. 15:3). (See also Job 11:11; 14:16; 34:22; Ps. 69:5; 90:8; Isa. 29:15; 65:12; Hos. 7:2; Amos 5:12.)

V. **The eyes of the Lord see all good.**
    "The eyes of the Lord are in every place, beholding the evil and the

good" (Prov. 15:3). (See also Ps. 33:18-19; 34:15; Jer. 24:6; I Peter 3:12.)

VI. **The eyes of the Lord try people.**

"The Lord is in his holy temple, the Lord's throne is in heaven: his eyes behold, his eyelids try, the children of men" (Ps. 11:4). He tests, or examines, every person.

VII. **The eyes of the Lord are looking everywhere for people who love Him.**

"For the eyes of the Lord run to and fro throughout the whole earth, to shew himself strong in the behalf of them whose heart is perfect toward him. . . ." (II Chron. 16:9).

The Lord is searching for people "whose heart is perfect toward him," who are wholeheartedly for Him, and when He finds people like that, He will "shew himself strong" in their behalf.

As the Lord sees and tries you and all your ways, does He see a person who loves Him wholeheartedly? If so, He will show Himself strong in your behalf and you will experience the truth of Psalm 84:11. "For the Lord God is a sun and shield: the Lord will give peace and glory: no good thing will he withhold from them that walk uprightly."

If, on the other hand, as the Lord sees you, He sees an unsaved person living in sin, you can pray like David: "O God, thou knowest my foolishness; and my sins are not hid from thee" (Ps. 69:5). Then, repent of your sins (Luke 13:3), receive the Lord Jesus Christ as your personal Saviour and Lord (John 1:12), and the Lord will save you (Rom. 10:9, 13).

> You cannot hide from God,
> Tho mountains cover you,
> His eye our secret thoughts behold,
> His mercies all our lives enfold,
> He knows our purposes untold,
> You cannot hide from God.
>
> You cannot hide from God,
> This one thing you can do,
> If you would save your sinful soul,
> If you would be made pure and whole,
> If you would reach the highest goal,
> Your soul must hide in God.

A. H. Ackley

16

THE LORD LOOKETH
ON THE HEART

I Samuel 16:7

The Bible has a lot to say about the heart. The words *heart* and *hearts* are used about 900 times in the Word of God. In most of these occurrences *heart* or *hearts* refers to the real person—the intellect, emotion, and will; man's entire mental and moral activity; the hidden springs of the personal life.

Speaking of Eliab, God said to Samuel, "Look not on his countenance, or on the height of his stature; because I have refused him: for the Lord seeth not as man seeth; for man looketh on the outward appearance, but the Lord looketh on the heart" (I Sam. 16:7). The Lord looks on the heart and:

> "pondereth" (Prov. 21:2; 24:12).
>
> "searches" (Jer. 17:10).
>
> "triest" (I Chron. 29:17).
>
> "knoweth" (Ps. 44:21).
>
> "understandeth all the imaginations of the thoughts"
> (I Chron. 28:9).
>
> "opens" (Acts 16:14).
>
> "establishes" (I Thess. 3:13).

The Lord looks into the heart of the unsaved.

I. **What He sees.**

A. A heart full of evil. ". . . The heart of the sons of men is full of evil. . . ." (Eccles. 9:3). (See also Eccles. 8:11; Gen. 6:5; Mark 7:21-23.)

B. A heart deceitful and desperately wicked. "The heart is deceitful above all things, and desperately wicked. . . ." (Jer. 17:9).

C. A hard heart. "Yea, they made their hearts as an adamant stone. . . ." (Zech. 7:12). (See also Mark 3:5; Heb. 3:7-8, 15.)

D. A deceived heart. "The pride of thine heart hath deceived thee" (Obad. 1:3).

E. A proud heart. ". . . Him that hath an high look and a proud heart will not I suffer" (Ps. 101:5).

F. A foolish heart. ". . . Their foolish heart was darkened" (Rom. 1:21).

G. A rebellious heart. "But this people hath a revolting and a rebellious heart. . . ." (Jer. 5:23).

H. A heart far from God. ". . . Their heart is far from me" (Matt. 15:8).

I. An unbelieving heart. ". . . An evil heart of unbelief. . . ." (Heb. 3:12).

J. A double heart. "Their heart is divided. . . ." (Hos. 10:2). (See also Psalm 12:2.)

II. **What He wants to see.**

A. A heart full of good. "A good man out of the good treasure of the heart bringeth forth good things. . . ." (Matt. 12:35).

B. An upright heart. "Light is sown for the righteous, and gladness for the upright in heart" (Ps. 97:11).

C. A soft heart. "For God maketh my heart soft, and the Almighty troubleth me" (Job 23:16).

D. A true heart. "Let us draw near with a true heart in full assurance of faith. . . ." (Heb. 10:22).

E. A humble heart. "I dwell in the high and holy place, with him also that is of a contrite and humble spirit, to revive the spirit of the humble, and to revive the heart of the contrite ones" (Isa. 57:15).

F. A wise heart. "The wise in heart will receive commandments. . . ." (Prov. 10:8).

G. An obedient heart. "But God be thanked, that ye were the servants of sin, but ye have obeyed from the heart that form of doctrine which was delivered you" (Rom. 6:17).

H. A heart seeking God. "And ye shall seek me, and find me, when ye shall search for me with all your heart" (Jer. 29:13).

I. A believing heart. "That if thou shalt confess with thy mouth the Lord Jesus, and shalt believe in thine heart that God hath raised him from the dead, thou shalt be saved" (Rom. 10:9). (See also Prov. 3:5-6; Acts 8:37.)

J. A single heart. "Servants, obey in all things your masters according to the flesh; not with eyeservice, as menpleasers; but in singleness of heart, fearing God" (Col. 3:22). (See also I Sam. 12:24; Ps. 9:1; 119:10, 69, 145; Matt. 22:37; Acts 2:46; Eph. 6:5-6.)

Let me ask you the question which Jehu put to Jehonadab. "Is thine heart right?" I pray that you can answer, as Jehonadab did: "It is" (II Kings 10:15).

Beware if it must be said of you as it was of Simon: ". . . Thy heart is not right in the sight of God" (Acts 8:21). If you will repent of your sins and believe on the Lord Jesus Christ (Luke 13:3; Acts 16:31), God will touch your heart (I Sam. 10:26), purify your heart by faith (Acts 15:9), and will say unto you, "A new heart also will I give you, and a new spirit will I put within you: and I will take away the stony heart out of your flesh, and I will give you an heart of flesh" (Ezek. 36:26).

17

THE MOST WICKED MAN
IN THE BIBLE

II Chronicles 33:1-19

Some students of the Bible believe that Manasseh is the most wicked man to be found in Scripture. The *Pilgrim Bible* notes: "This name means *Making to forget*. He was the worst king of Judah. . . ." As we study our text we learn much about this wicked man.

I. His sins.

  A. He did that which was evil in the sight of the Lord (v. 2). "But did that which was evil in the sight of the Lord. . . ."

  B. He was an idolator (vv. 3-5).

    1. "He built again the high places" (v. 3).
    2. "He reared up altars for Baalim" (v. 3).
    3. "Made groves" (v. 3).
    4. "Worshipped all the host of heaven, and served them" (v. 3).
    5. "He built altars in the house of the Lord" (v. 4).
    6. "He built altars for all the host of heaven in the two courts of the house of the Lord" (v. 5).

  C. He murdered his children (v. 6).

    "And he caused his children to pass through the fire in the valley of the son of Hinnom. . . ."

    He offered his own children as a sacrifice to the pagan god Molech. This pagan sacrifice could have involved his children in either passing between two fires as an act of dedication to

Molech or in actually passing through the fire as a human sacrifice to this pagan god. This was forbidden by God in Leviticus 18:21. "And thou shalt not let any of thy seed [children] pass through the fire to Molech."

D. He practiced magic and witchcraft (v. 6).

"... He observed times [watched for certain signs instead of seeking God's will], and used enchantments, and used witchcraft, and dealt with a familiar spirit [a demon spirit], and with wizards...."

All of this was forbidden by God in Deuteronomy 18:9-12.

E. He desecrated the house of God (v. 7).

"And he set a carved image, the idol which he had made, in the house of God...."

F. He caused his people to sin (v. 9).

"So Manasseh made Judah and the inhabitants of Jerusalem to err, and to do worse than the heathen."

G. He shed innocent blood (II Kings 21:16).

"Moreover Manasseh shed innocent blood very much, till he had filled Jerusalem from one end to another...."

A note on "they were sawn asunder" in Hebrews 11:37 in the *Pilgrim Bible* explains: "Tradition, both Jewish and Christian, says that Isaiah was thus martyred...."

II. His salvation.

In spite of the fact that he was such a notoriously wicked man, we believe that the Bible makes it clear that he was saved from his sins.

A. The Lord spoke to Manasseh (vv. 10, 18).

"And the Lord spake to Manasseh.... The words of the seers that spake to him in the name of the Lord God of Israel...."

B. The Lord afflicted him (vv. 11-12).

"Wherefore the Lord brought upon them the captains of the host of the king of Assyria, which took Manasseh among the thorns, and bound him with fetters, and carried him to Babylon. And when he was in affliction...."

C. The Lord saved him (vv. 12-13).

1. "He besought the Lord" (v. 12).
2. "He humbled himself greatly before the God of his fathers" (v. 12).
3. He "prayed unto him" (v. 13).

4. The Lord "heard his supplication" (v. 13).

5. "Then Manasseh knew that the Lord he was God" (v. 13).

III. His service.

After God saved Manasseh, he became a changed man. He began to serve the Lord diligently.

A. He was brought back by the Lord "to Jerusalem into his kingdom" (v. 13).

B. "He built a wall without the city of David" (v. 14).

C. He put away idolatry (v. 15).

"And he took away the strange gods, and the idol out of the house of the Lord, and all the altars that he had built in the mount of the house of the Lord, and in Jerusalem, and cast them out of the city."

D. "He repaired the altar of the Lord" (v. 16).

E. He "sacrificed thereon peace offerings and thank offerings" (v. 16).

F. He "commanded Judah to serve the Lord God of Israel" (v. 16).

It is encouraging to know that God loves sinners and is willing and able to save the worst of them. He promises in Isaiah 1:18: "Come now, and let us reason together, saith the Lord: though your sins be as scarlet, they shall be as white as snow; though they be red like crimson, they shall be as wool."

Paul gives us a wonderful testimony. "This is a faithful saying, and worthy of all acception, that Christ Jesus came into the world to save sinners; of whom I am chief" (I Tim. 1:15).

No matter how wicked you are, there is good news for you from God: the most wicked man in the Bible was saved; the chief of sinners was saved; and you can be saved!

If you will humble yourself before the Lord and call upon Him, He promises: "For whosoever shall call upon the name of the Lord shall be saved" (Rom. 10:13). The Lord Jesus Christ has already paid for all your sins and as you repent and believe on Him (Luke 13:3; Acts 16:31), He will save you from every sin and "the blood of Jesus Christ his Son cleanseth us from all sin" (I John 1:7). Then with your sins forgiven and forgotten (Heb. 10:17), you can "serve him in truth with all your heart" (I Sam. 12:24).

18

THE RESULTS OF A GREAT SERMON

Acts 2:14-47

The sermon preached by Peter on the day of Pentecost, recorded in our Bible passage, is probably the most frequently used preaching model in the Bible. Peter proclaimed this message in Jerusalem immediately after the Holy Spirit came to baptize believers into the body of Christ, as promised by Jesus Christ in Acts 1:4-5. This great sermon could very well be a model for preachers today. Peter "lifted up his voice" and spoke of the:

1. person of Christ. "Jesus of Nazareth, a man approved of God among you" (v. 22a).

2. ministry of Christ. "Miracles and wonders and signs, which God did by him" (v. 22b).

3. death of Christ. "Him . . . ye have taken, and by wicked hands have crucified and slain" (v. 23).

4. resurrection of Christ. "Whom God hath raised up" (vv. 24-32).

5. ascension of Christ. "Therefore being by the right hand of God exalted" (v. 33a).

6. descent of the Holy Spirit. "Having received of the Father the promise of the Holy Ghost" (v. 33b).

7. lordship of Christ. ". . . God hath made that same Jesus . . . both Lord and Christ" (v. 36).

Now let us see the results of this great sermon.

I. **There was conviction.**

"Now when they heard this, they were pricked in their heart" (v. 37a).

This was the work of the Holy Spirit, who convicted them of their sin of crucifying the Son of God. Jesus had promised that when the Holy Spirit came, He would "reprove the world of sin, and of righteousness, and of judgment" (John 16:8).

II. **There was contrition.**

Those who were convicted of their sin showed contrition when they cried out: "Men and brethren, what shall we do?" (v. 37b).

III. **There was conversion.**

"Then they that gladly received his word. . . ." (v. 41a).

They received the written Word of God and the living Word of God, the Lord Jesus Christ. "But as many as received him, to them gave he power to become the sons of God, even to them that believe on his name" (John 1:12). "Being born again, not of corruptible seed, but of incorruptible, by the word of God, which liveth and abideth for ever" (I Peter 1:23).

IV. **There was confession.**

Those who were converted "were baptized" (v. 41a).

By their baptism they confessed their identification with the Lord Jesus Christ who had died for them, been buried, and had risen again from the dead. At least nine times in the Book of The Acts we read that people were converted and immediately were baptized: Acts 2:41; 8:12; 8:35-38; 9:18; 10:44-48; 16:14-15; 16:33; 18:8; 19:5.

V. **There was church membership.**

"And the same day there were added unto them about three thousand souls" (v. 41b).

These 3,000 people were added to the 120 who were baptized into the body of Christ that morning by the Holy Spirit (Acts 1:15; 2:1-4). Every person who is saved should unite with a Bible-believing local church. "Not forsaking the assembling of ourselves together, as the manner of some is; but exhorting one another: and so much the more, as ye see the day approaching" (Heb. 10:25).

VI. **There was continuance.**

"And they continued stedfastly
    in the apostles' doctrine
    and fellowship,

and in breaking of bread,
and in prayers" (v. 42).

They proved the reality of their discipleship by their continuance. Jesus said: "If ye continue in my word, then are ye my disciples indeed" (John 8:31). Paul exhorted Christians: "Therefore, my beloved brethren, be ye stedfast, unmoveable, always abounding in the work of the Lord, forasmuch as ye know that your labour is not in vain in the Lord" (I Cor. 15:58).

VII. **There was consecration.**

These Christians were truly consecrated. They displayed many Christian virtues:

A. Unity. "All that believed were together.... with one accord" (vv. 44, 46).

B. Love. "... Had all things common, and sold their possessions and goods, and parted them to all men, as every man had need" (vv. 44-45).

C. Joy. "... Did eat their meat with gladness" (v. 46).

D. Sincerity. "Singleness of heart" (v. 46).

E. Praise. "Praising God" (v. 47).

F. Favor. "Favour with all the people" (v. 47).

G. Growth. "... And the Lord added to the church daily such as should be saved" (v. 47).

They grew increasingly. "... And the number of the men was about five thousand" (Acts 4:4).

"And believers were the more *added* to the Lord, multitudes both of men and women" (Acts 5:14).

"And the word of God increased; and the number of the disciples *multiplied* in Jerusalem greatly; and a great company of the priests were obedient to the faith" (Acts 6:7).

Let us who preach pray that God may be pleased to use our sermons to bring the same results as those which took place on that great day of Pentecost. Amen!

19

THREE THINGS TO CONSIDER

Haggai 1:5-7
Deuteronomy 32:29
Hebrews 3:1

There are a number of things which God tells us to consider:

> the "heavens" (Ps. 8:3).
> "the poor" (Ps. 41:1).
> the "ways" of the ant (Prov. 6:6).
> the "lilies of the field" (Matt. 6:28).
> "the ravens" (Luke 12:24).
> "thyself" (Gal. 6:1).
> "one another" (Heb. 10:24).

God laments in Isaiah 1:3: ". . . My people doth not consider." I pray this will not have to be said of you, but rather that you are a person who does consider. Here are three things to consider.

I. **Consider your sin.**

A few thousand Israelites had returned from Babylon to Palestine after spending seventy years in captivity there. They had started rebuilding their temple, but had become discouraged because of the opposition of their enemies, and had stopped the work on their temple (Ezra 4). God sent the prophets Haggai, Zechariah, and Malachi to preach to them, to stir them up to finish God's work.

Haggai preached to them about dwelling in their fine houses, and neglecting God's house (Hag. 1:3-11). Twice in that message he exhorted them, *"Consider your ways"* (vv. 5, 7). They were guilty of the sin of putting other things before God's work, and because of this, God was bringing judgment upon them by withholding blessing from them (vv. 6, 9-11).

God says in Jeremiah 48:10: "Cursed be he that doeth the work of the Lord deceitfully [negligently] . . . ." Jesus commands us today, "But seek ye first the kingdom of God, and his righteousness. . . ." (Matt. 6:33). If you are guilty of negligence in doing God's work and putting other things before His work, may God help you to consider your sin and turn from it.

As Haggai preached to them, they considered their sin and did something about it.

A. They obeyed.

"Then Zerubbabel the son of Shealtiel, and Joshua the son of Josedech, the high priest, with all the remnant of the people, obeyed the voice of the Lord their God, and the words of Haggai the prophet. . . . (v. 12).

B. They feared the Lord.

". . . And the people did fear before the Lord" (v. 12).

C. They were stirred.

"And the Lord stirred up the spirit of Zerubbabel . . . and the spirit of Joshua . . . and the spirit of all the remnant of the people. . . . (v. 14).

D. They did God's work.

". . . And they came and did work in the house of the Lord of hosts, their God" (v. 14).

Consider your sin and do something about it:

be obedient to the Lord (Acts 5:29).
fear the Lord (Heb. 12:28).
be stirred by the Lord (II Tim. 1:6).
do the Lord's work (Matt. 21:28).

II. Consider your soul.

God's desire for all men is given in Deuteronomy 32:29: "O that they were wise, that they understood this, that they would *consider their latter end!*" David prayed: "Lord, make me to know mine end. . . ." (Ps. 39:4).

Every person should consider where he will spend eternity. Jesus Christ asked this very important question, "For what shall it profit a man, if he shall gain the whole world, and lose his own soul?" (Mark 8:36).

My friend, please consider your soul—where will you be when you leave this earth? According to the Word of God, there are only two places to go after we leave this earth—Heaven or Hell. If your soul is saved through a real faith in the Lord Jesus Christ, you will go to Heaven (John 14:1-6). God will give you everlasting life, and you will forever be with the Lord (Rom. 6:23; I Thess. 4:17).

If you are not saved, you will go to Hell when you die (Luke 16:22-23), and you will forever be separated from the Lord (Rev. 14:10-11; 20:11-15; 21:8).

> Eternity, eternity, where will you spend eternity?
> It's Heaven or Hell for you and me,
> Where will you spend eternity?

Anonymous

III. Consider your Saviour.

"Wherefore, holy brethren, partakers of the heavenly calling, *consider* the Apostle and High Priest of our profession, *Christ Jesus*" (Heb. 3:1).

Here we are told to consider the Saviour, the Lord Jesus Christ. God commands us to "lay aside every weight, and the sin which doth so easily beset us, and let us run with patience the race that is set before us, looking unto Jesus the author and finisher of our faith; who for the joy that was set before him endured the cross, despising the shame, and is set down at the right hand of the throne of God. For *consider him* that endured such contradiction of sinners against himself, lest ye be wearied and faint in your minds" (Heb. 12:1-3).

We should consider Him and what He endured for us to purchase our salvation. Samuel gave good advice when he said: "Only fear the Lord, and serve him in truth with all your heart: for *consider how great things he hath done for you*" (I Sam. 12:24). Here are just a few things He did or endured for you and me.

A. He left Heaven to come to earth (John 6:38).

B. He became "poor" (II Cor. 8:9).

C. He was born in a stable (Luke 2:7).

D. He had nowhere "to lay His head" (Matt. 8:20).

E. He did not accumulate possessions (Matt. 17:24-27).

F. He was rejected by His own "brethren" (John 7:5).

G. He was called many evil names and accused of much wrongdoing.

> "Gluttonous, and a winebibber" (Matt. 11:19).
> "A Samaritan, and hast a devil" (John 8:48).

"Not of God" (John 9:16).
"Sinner" (John 9:24).
"Blasphemer" (John 10:33).

H. He was thought to be "beside himself" (Mark 3:20-21).

I. He was accused of casting out demons by "Beelzebub, the prince of the devils" (Matt. 12:22-24).

J. He was almost stoned (John 8:59; 10:31).

K. He was rejected by the people of several cities.
Bethlehem (Luke 2:7).
Nazareth (Matt. 13:54-58; Luke 4:16-30).
Chorazin and Bethsaida (Matt. 11:20-22).
Gadara (Mark 5:1-17).
Jerusalem (Matt. 23:37-38; Luke 19:41-44).

L. He was hated by the Pharisees, Sadducees, scribes, elders, and chief priests (Matt. 12:14, 24; 26:3-4).

M. He was betrayed by Judas (Matt. 26:47-50).

N. He was denied by Peter (Matt. 26:69-75).

O. He was forsaken by all (Matt. 26:56).

P. He was crowned with "thorns" (Matt. 27:29-30).

Q. He was beaten and spit upon (Matt. 26:67; 27:30; Isa. 50:6; 52:14).

R. His back was beaten (Matt. 27:26; Ps. 129:3).

S. His hands and feet were nailed to the cross and His side was pierced (Ps. 22:16; John 19:34).

T. His bones were "out of joint" (Ps. 22:14).

U. His heart was "broken" (Ps. 69:20).

V. His life was given and His blood was shed (John 10:11, 18; I Peter 1:18-19).

W. His soul was made "an offering for sin," and God "made him to be sin for us" (Isa. 53:10; II Cor. 5:21).

X. He was "forsaken" by God (Matt. 27:46).

Y. He was "made a curse for us" (Gal. 3:13).

Z. He paid the full price of sin for us (John 19:30; Rom. 5:8; I Cor. 15:3-4).

As I think of all that my Saviour has done for me, I exclaim with Isaac Watts:

> Were the whole realm of nature mine,
> That were a present far too small;
> Love so amazing, so divine
> Demands my soul, my life, my all.

May this be your response too as you consider your sin, your soul, and your Saviour; and may you receive Him (John 1:12), love Him (I John 4:19), and live for Him (II Cor. 5:14-15).

20

THREE WORTHY AMBITIONS

II Corinthians 5:9
I Thessalonians 4:11-12
Romans 15:20

Describing a film director, Paul D. Zimmerman observed in *Newsweek* magazine: "[He] is something of an unguided missile, loaded with talent, but not yet pointed in any firm direction."

Speaking to the Canadian Club, Dr. Hans Selye, director of the Institute of Experimental Medicine and Surgery at the University of Montreal, claimed that aimlessness is one of the worst problems plaguing today's world. Many young people, he said, don't think anything is worth doing, "and that is a horrible blow to humanity."

Many people have no ambitions, and many others have unworthy ambitions. Some men seek fame, or wealth, or success. God's Word speaks of unworthy ambitions. "And seekest thou great things for thyself? seek them not. . . ." (Jer. 45:5). We are not to seek great things for ourselves, but we should seek great things for God. William Carey put it well: "Attempt great things for God; expect great things from God."

Henry Wadsworth Longfellow said. "Many people would succeed in small things if they were not troubled with great ambitions."

A. T. Robertson, a Greek scholar, remarked: "A preacher devoid of ambition lacks power." Of course, he was speaking of ambition which is worthy.

The Greek verb *philotimeomai* occurs three times in the New Testament. In translating these three occurrences, three different English words are used in the Authorized Version. This Greek word could also be translated "to be ambitious" in each of these instances. Here are the three worthy ambitions spoken of in the New Testament.

I. Be ambitious to please Christ.

Paul speaks of a worthy ambition. "Wherefore we labour, that, whether present or absent, we may be accepted of him" (II Cor. 5:9). The word *labour* here comes from the Greek word *philotimeomai,* and the words *accepted of* could be translated *well pleasing to.* So this verse is really saying that Paul was ambitious to be well pleasing to Christ. One version renders it: "We are constantly ambitious and strive earnestly to be wellpleasing to Him." Bengel said that this is "the sole legitimate ambition."

In Revelation 4:10-11 we read that the four and twenty elders cast their crowns before the Lord and say: "Thou art worthy, O Lord, to receive glory and honour and power: for thou hast created all things, and *for thy pleasure they are and were created.*" All things and all people have been created for God's pleasure or to bring pleasure to Him.

In order to please the Lord, the Bible says we must be:

A. Saved.

"So then they that are in the flesh cannot *please* God" (Rom. 8:8). "But without faith it is impossible to *please* him. . . ." (Heb. 11:6). A person cannot be well pleasing to the Lord until he has trusted Jesus Christ as his personal Saviour.

B. Surrendered.

Even after a person is saved, he still cannot please the Lord as he should until he is surrendered to God. "I beseech you therefore, brethren, by the mercies of God, that ye present your bodies a living sacrifice, holy, acceptable unto God, which is your reasonable service" (Rom. 12:1). The phrase "acceptable unto God" could be translated "well pleasing to God." Only as a Christian is surrendered to the Lord can he be pleasing to Him.

C. Serving.

Paul spoke of the gospel in terms of his responsibility to God. "But as we were allowed of God to be put in trust with the gospel, even so we speak; not as *pleasing* men, but *God,* which trieth our hearts" (I Thess. 2:4). We, too, have been put in trust with the gospel, and should give it to others as we serve Him. Jesus Christ said: ". . . I do always those things that *please* Him" (John 8:29).

May our testimony be that of Enoch. ". . . He had this testimony, that he *pleased* God" (Heb. 11:5).

II. Be ambitious to portray Christ.

Paul told the Christians at Thessalonica: "And that ye study to be quiet, and to do your own business, and to work with your own hands, as we commanded you; That ye may walk honestly toward them that are without, and that ye may have lack of nothing" (I Thess. 4:11-12). The word *study* here comes from the Greek word *philotimeomai;* so the first part of verse 11 could be translated "and that ye be ambitious to be quiet." God is saying to Christians that they should be ambitious to live in such an exemplary way that those "that are without" (the unsaved) would see Christ in them, or, in other words, that they might portray Christ to others.

> O to reflect His grace,
> Causing the world to see
> Love that will glow,
> 'Till others shall know
> Jesus, revealed in me.
>
> *Gipsy Smith*

III. Be ambitious to preach Christ.

Paul wrote of a third worthy ambition. "Yea, so have I strived to preach the gospel, not where Christ was named, lest I should build upon another man's foundation" (Rom. 15:20). The word *strived* here comes from the Greek word *philotimeomai;* so Paul is saying that he is ambitious to preach the gospel to those who have never heard of Christ. Surely, this is a most worthy ambition, one which every Christian should have. Jesus commanded us: "Go ye into all the world, and preach the gospel to every creature" (Mark 16:15). There are many people all about us in this country and millions in other countries who have not heard the gospel. We are told that more than half of the world's population have never heard a clear presentation of the gospel of Jesus Christ.

David Brainerd had this ambition: "I cared not where or how I lived, or what hardships I endured so that I could but gain souls for Christ. While I was asleep I dreamt of such things, and when I waked the first thing I thought of was winning souls to Christ."

George Whitefield was ambitious to preach Christ. He said: "If God did not give me souls, I believe I would die."

73

When King Edward VII asked William Booth to write in his autograph album, the old man—now seventy-five—bent forward, took the pen, and summed up his life's work.

> Your Majesty,
> Some men's ambition is art,
> Some men's ambition is fame,
> Some men's ambition is gold,
> My ambition is the souls of men.

My prayer is that we may be ambitious to be well pleasing to Christ, to portray Christ, and to preach Him.

21

WHAT DOES IT MEAN
TO BE LOST?

Luke 19:10

There are really only two classes of people in the world—the saved and the lost. Every person is in one or the other of these classes; there is no middle ground. Many people do not realize this, and consequently they are not concerned about themselves.

Jesus made it clear that there were only two classes. "He that believeth on him [Christ] is not condemned: but he that believeth not is condemned already, because he hath not believed in the name of the only begotten Son of God" (John 3:18). Notice that Christ said "he that believeth not is *condemned already.*" A person who has not truly believed on Jesus Christ does not have to do another thing to be lost—he is lost already.

When a person is lost physically, he is not where he belongs; he has no sense of direction; he cannot find his way; he is away from those who love him; he is away from those who are seeking him; he is away from home. This is also true of a person who is lost spritually.

Rev. William Arnot wrote in *Laws From Heaven For Life On Earth*: "Every soul not already won to Jesus is already lost." James M. Gray, a lost man, read this statement, was convicted by it, and received Christ as his personal Saviour. He later became the president of Moody Bible Institute in Chicago.

Lost sinners need to understand what it means to be lost so that they will want to be saved. Christians also need to understand what it means to be lost so that they will have a compassionate concern for the salvation of the lost.

The New Testament reveals that there is a wide variation, or degree, of sinfulness, but there is no variation concerning the state of sinfulness. Here is the teaching of the Bible concerning what it means to be lost.

I. You Cannot See the Kingdom of God (John 3:3).

II. You Cannot Enter into the Kingdom of God (John 3:5).

III. You Cannot Understand Spiritual Things (John 3:5; I Cor. 2:14).

IV. You Will Perish (John 3:15-16; I Cor. 1:18; II Peter 3:9).

V. You Are Condemned Already (John 3:18).

VI. You Love Darkness Rather than Light (John 3:19a).

VII. Your Deeds Were Evil (John 3:19b).

VIII. You Hate the Light (John 3:20).

IX. You Do Not Come to the Light (John 3:20).

X. You Do Not Want Your Deeds Reproved (John 3:20).

XI. You Shall Not See Life (John 3:36).

XII. You Have the Wrath of God Abiding on You (John 3:36).

XIII. You Are Under Sin (Rom. 3:9).

XIV. You Are Not Righteous (Rom. 3:10).

XV. You Do Not Understand (Rom 3:11a).

XVI. You Do Not Seek God (Rom. 3:11b).

XVII. You Are Gone out of the Way (Rom. 3:12a).

XVIII. You Are Unprofitable (Rom. 3:12b).

XIX. You Don't Do Good (Rom. 3:12c).

XX. Your Throat Is an Open Sepulchre (Rom. 3:13a).

XXI. You Have a Tongue Which Uses Deceit (Rom. 3:13b).

XXII. You Have the Poison of Asps Under Your Lips (Rom. 3:13c).

XXIII. You Have a Mouth Full of Cursing and Bitterness (Rom. 3:14).

XXIV. You Have Feet Swift to Shed Blood (Rom. 3:15).

XXV. You Have Destruction and Misery in Your Ways (Rom. 3:16).

XXVI. You Don't Know the Way of Peace (Rom. 3:17).

XXVII. You Have No Fear of God Before Your Eyes (Rom. 3:18).

XXVIII. You Are Guilty Before God (Rom. 3:19).

XXIX. You Are Dead in Trespasses and Sins (Eph. 2:1).

XXX. You Walk According to the Course of This World (Eph. 2:2a).

XXXI. You Walk According to the Prince of the Power of the Air (Satan) (Eph. 2:2b).

XXXII. You Live in the Lusts of Your Flesh (Eph. 2:3a).

XXXIII. You Are a Child of Wrath (Eph. 2:3a).

XXXIV. You Are Without Christ (Eph. 2:12a).

XXXV. You Are an Alien from the Commonwealth of Israel (Eph. 2:12b).

XXXVI. You Are a Stranger from the Covenants of Promise (Eph. 2:12c).

XXXVII. You Have No Hope (Eph. 2:12d).

XXXVIII. You Are Without God in the World (Eph. 2:12e).

XXXIX. You Are Far Off (Eph. 2:13).

XL. You Are Foolish, Disobedient, Deceived, Serving Divers Lusts and Pleasures, Living in Malice and Envy, Hateful, and Hating Others (Titus 3:3).

XLI. You Are Walking on the Broad Way That Leads to Destruction (Matt. 7:13).

XLII. You Are Against Christ (Matt. 12:30).

XLIII. You Cannot Worship God Acceptably (John 4:22-24; Acts 17:23).

XLIV. You Dishonor the Father (John 5:23).

XLV. You Are the Servant of Sin (John 8:34).

XLVI. You Are at Enmity with God (Rom. 5:10; 8:7).

XLVII. You Cannot Please God (Rom. 8:8; Heb. 11:6).

XLVIII. You Cannot Go Where Christ Is (John 7:34; 8:21, 24).

XLIX. You Are Blinded by Satan (II Cor. 4:3-4).

L. You Are in Darkness and Under the Power of Satan (Acts 26:18).

LI. You Resist the Holy Spirit (Acts 7:51).

LII. You Harden Your Heart and Treasure Up unto Yourself Wrath (Rom. 2:5).

LIII. You Do Not Have Faith and Therefore Everything You Do Is Sin (Rom. 14:23).

LIV. You Will Receive the Wages of Sin Which Is Death–Physical, Spiritual, and Eternal (Rom. 6:23).

LV. You Will Be Judged and Cast into the Lake of Fire for All Eternity (Rev. 20:11-15).

This list could be made longer. May God help those of us who are Christians to study these facts concerning the lost, and realize that all around us are lost people who are in danger of going to Hell forever. Let us ponder the words of R. A. Torrey: "Meditate upon it in its practical, personal bearings, until your heart is burdened by the awful peril of the wicked and you rush out to spend the last dollar, if need be, and the last ounce of strength you have, in saving those imperiled men from the certain, awful Hell of conscious agony and shame to which they are fast hurrying."

Lost person, there is good news for you in our text. "For the Son of man [Jesus Christ] is come to seek and to save that which was lost." Thank God, "Christ Jesus came into the world to save sinners" (I Tim. 1:15). Jesus Christ has paid for your sins when He died on the cross (I Peter 2:24; 3:18), and He offers to save you if you will repent of your sins and believe on Him (Luke 13:3; Acts 16:31).

When you receive Him as your personal Saviour, you can say what the little country boy said. A traveling salesman was inquiring about the distance and direction to the next town. The boy was timid and backward, and his answer to each question was: "I don't know." The salesman became angry and said, "Well, don't you know anything?" "Yes," said the boy, "I know where I'm going and I know I'm not lost!"

22

WHAT DOES IT MEAN
TO BE SAVED?

Acts 16:30-31

According to the Bible, people are either saved or lost. Paul said in I Cor. 1:18: "For the preaching of the cross is to them that perish foolishness; but unto us which are saved it is the power of God." He mentions only two classes—"them that perish" and "us which are saved."

The word *salvation* encompasses all that God does for man in delivering him from sin and its effects. The word is used 164 times in the Bible—119 times in the Old Testament and 45 times in the New Testament. Salvation comes from God. ". . . Salvation is of the Lord" (Jonah 2:9).

Salvation is in three tenses—past, present, and future.

Past tense. This means to be saved from the penalty of sin, or *justification* (Luke 7:50; Acts 16:31; I Cor. 1:18; Eph. 2:8-9; II Tim. 1:9).

Present tense. This means to be saved from the power of sin, or *santification* (Rom. 6:14; Phil. 2:12-13).

Future tense. This means to be saved from the presence of sin, or *glorification* (Rom. 13:11).

C. I. Scofield has given an excellent definition of salvation.

Salvation is that work of God—Father, Son, and Holy Spirit— whereby the believer in the Lord Jesus Christ is redeemed from the curse of the law, justified, kept, set free from the dominion of sin, sanctified, and finally perfected in the image of his Lord.

Our text asks and answers the most important question in the world: ". . . What must I do to be saved? And they said, Believe on the Lord Jesus Christ and thou shalt be saved, and thy house." When a person truly believes on the Lord Jesus Christ with his heart and calls on the Lord, he is saved (Rom. 10:9-10, 13). If you are saved, here are some of the things God has done for you. This is what it means to be saved.

    I.   You Have Been Foreknown by God (Rom. 8:29; I Peter 1:2).

    II.   You Have Been Predestinated by God (Rom. 8:29; Eph. 1:5, 11).

    III.   You Have Been Called by God (Rom. 8:30).

    IV.   You Have Been Justified by God (Rom. 8:30; Rom 5:1).

    V.   You Have Been Convicted by the Holy Spirit (John 16:7-11).

    VI.   You Have Been Drawn by God (John 6:44, 65).

    VII.   You Have Had Your Heart Opened by God (Acts 16:14).

    VIII.   You Have Been Given to Christ by God (John 6:37; 17:3, 6, 12).

    IX.   You Have Been Redeemed (Eph. 1:7; Col. 1:14; Heb. 9:12; I Peter 1:18-19).

    X.   You Have Been Reconciled (Rom. 5:10; II Cor. 5:18-19; Col. 1:20).

    XI.   You Have Been Granted Repentance (Acts 5:31; 11:18; II Tim. 2:25).

    XII.   You Have Been Given Faith (Acts 13:48; Eph. 2:8-9).

    XIII.   You Have Been Forgiven (Eph. 1:7; Acts 10:43; 13:38-39; I John 2:12).

    XIV.   You Have Been Regenerated (John 1:12-13; 3:3-7; Titus 3:5).

    XV.   You Have Been Sanctified (I Cor. 1:30; Heb. 10:10, 14).

    XVI.   You Have Been Perfected Forever (Heb. 10:14).

    XVII.   You Have Been Baptized by the Holy Spirit into the Body of Christ (I Cor. 12:13).

    XVIII.   You Have Been Sealed by the Holy Spirit (Eph. 1:13; 4:30).

    XIX.   You Have Been Made the Temple of the Holy Spirit (I Cor. 6:19).

    XX.   You Have Been Given Eternal Life (John 3:16; 5:24; 10:27-29; Rom. 6:23; I John 5:11-13).

    XXI.   You Have Become a Child of God (John 1:12).

    XXII.   You Have Been Made Free (John 8:36; Rom. 8:2).

    XXIII.   You Have Been Given Rest (Matt. 11:28).

    XXIV.   You Have Been Washed from Your Sins (Rev. 1:5).

    XXV.   You Have Been Brought into Vital Union with Jesus Christ (John 15:1-7; Rom. 6:3-8).

XXVI.	You Have Had Your Spiritual Eyes Opened (Acts 26:18).
XXVII.	You Have Been Turned from Darkness to Light (Acts 26:18).
XXVIII.	You Have Been Turned from the Power of Satan unto God (Acts 26:18).
XXIX.	You Have Become a Saint (Rom. 1:7; I Cor. 1:2).
XXX.	You Have Been Delivered from Condemnation (John 3:18; 5:24; Rom. 8:1; I Cor. 11:32).
XXXI.	You Have Been Given Peace (John 14:27; Rom. 5:1; Eph. 2:14, 17).
XXXII.	You Have Been Made a New Creation (II Cor. 5:17; Gal. 6:15).
XXXIII.	You Have Been Delivered from This Present Evil Age (Gal. 1:4).
XXXIV.	You Have Been Delivered from the Curse of the Law (Gal. 3:13).
XXXV.	You Have Been Made an Heir of God and a Joint Heir with Jesus Christ (Rom. 8:16-17).
XXXVI.	You Have Been Taken into the Hands of Christ and His Father for Safekeeping (John 10:27-30).
XXXVII.	You Have Been Raised Up and Made to Sit in the Heavenlies with Christ (Eph. 2:6).
XXXVIII.	You Have Obtained an Inheritance (Eph. 1:11; I Peter 1:3-4).
XXXIX.	You Have Been Made Nigh by the Blood of Christ (Eph. 2:13).
XL.	You Have Christ Living in You (II Cor. 13:5; Gal. 2:20; Col. 1:27; Rev. 3:20).
XLI.	You Have Been Given Access into God's Grace (Rom. 5:2).
XLII.	You Have Been Made Abraham's Spiritual Seed (Gal. 3:29).
XLIII.	You Have Been Adopted into the Family of God (Rom. 8:15, 23; Eph. 1:5).
XLIV.	You Have A Saviour Who Intercedes for You (Rom. 8:34; Heb. 7:25).
XLV.	You Have Been Made Alive (Eph. 2:1).
XLVI.	You Have Been Translated into the Kingdom of God's Son (Col. 1:13).
XLVII.	You Have Been Made Complete in Christ (Col. 2:10).
XLVIII.	You Have Been Made a Chosen Generation, a Royal Priesthood, an Holy Nation, a Peculiar People (I Peter 2:9).
XLIX.	You Have Been Made Accepted in the Beloved (Eph. 1:6).
L.	You Have Been Made Meet (Fit) to Be Partakers of the Inheritance of the Saints in Light (Col. 1:12).
LI.	You Have Been Made His Workmanship (Masterpiece) (Eph. 2:10).

LII. You Have Been Made a Worker Together with God (I Cor. 3:9).

LIII. You Have Become an Ambassador for Christ (II Cor. 5:20).

LIV. You Have Become a Fellow Citizen with the Saints, and of the Household of God (Eph. 2:19).

LV. You Have Become Light in the Lord (Eph. 5:8).

LVI. You Have Become a Member in His Body (I Cor. 12:13).

LVII. You Have Become a Stone in the Building (Eph. 2:19-22; I Peter 2:5).

LVIII. You Have Become a Sheep in the Flock (John 10:27-29).

LIX. You Have Become a Part of His Bride (Eph. 5:25-27, 32).

LX. You Have Been Made a Branch in the Vine (John 15:5).

LXI. You Have Been Made a Priest of the Kingdom of Priests (I Peter 2:5, 9; Rev. 1:6).

LXII. You Have Been Given All Things That Pertain unto Life and Godliness (II Peter 1:3).

LXIII. You Have Been Given All Things to Enjoy (I Tim. 6:17).

LXIV. You Have the Promise of Glorification (Rom. 8:30).

LXV. You Have Been Blessed with All Spiritual Blessings in the Heavenlies in Christ (Eph. 1:3).

All these wonderful blessings are true of every person who is saved. If you are saved, rejoice because of them and thank Him for all He has done for you and what He shall yet do for you.

If you are not saved, "now is the accepted time; behold, now is the day of salvation" (II Cor. 6:2). Call upon the Lord and He promises: "For whosoever shall call upon the name of the Lord shall be saved" (Rom. 10:13). Then you too can rejoice in these blessings, and know what it means to be saved.

23

WHO IS ON THE LORD'S SIDE?

Exodus 32:36

When Moses came down from Mount Sinai where he had been with God for forty days, he saw the people of Israel dancing around a golden calf. He became angry, destroyed their idol, and stood before them and asked, "Who is on the Lord's side?"

Jesus Christ made it plain that everyone is either on the Lord's side or the devil's side. "He that is not with me is against me; and he that gathereth not with me scattereth abroad" (Matt. 12:30).

During the Civil War a prayer was suggested to the president. "Mr. Lincoln, let us pray that the Lord will be on our side." The president replied: "I am not concerned that the Lord be on our side. My concern is that we be on the Lord's side."

My concern is that you be on the Lord's side. I want to ask and answer three questions in this message.

I. **What does it mean to be on the Lord's side?**

Everyone is born in sin and wants his own way. "All we like sheep have gone astray; we have turned every one to his own way. . . ." (Isa. 53:6). To get on the Lord's side we have to turn from our own way to God's way.

A. We must repent to get on the Lord's side. Jesus said: ". . . Except ye repent, ye shall all likewise perish" (Luke 13:3). Paul said that God "commandeth all men every where to repent" (Acts 17:30). He also testified concerning "repentance toward God, and faith toward our Lord Jesus Christ" (Acts 20:21). He told King Agrippa that people "should repent and turn to God, and do works meet for repentance" (Acts 26:20).

B. We must believe on the Lord Jesus Christ to get on the Lord's side. Jesus said: ". . . Repent ye, and believe the gospel" (Mark 1:15). The question is asked in Acts 16:30: "Sirs, what must I do to be saved?" The answer is given in the next verse. "Believe on the Lord Jesus Christ, and thou shalt be saved, and thy house" (Acts 16:31). Romans 10:9 refers to believing with the heart: "That if thou shalt confess with thy mouth the Lord Jesus, and shalt believe in thine heart that God hath raised him from the dead, thou shalt be saved."

When a person repents and believes on the Lord Jesus Christ, he leaves the devil's side and is now on the Lord's side. To show others we are on the Lord's side there are certain things we should do.

C. We should confess Jesus Christ with our mouth to let people know we are on the Lord's side.

"Whosoever therefore shall confess me before men, him will I confess also before my Father which is in heaven. But whosoever shall deny me before men, him will I also deny before my Father which is in heaven" (Matt. 10:32-33).

D. We should confess Jesus Christ in our baptism to let people know we are on the Lord's side.

Christ gave His church the Great Commission. "Go ye therefore, and teach [disciple] all nations, baptizing them in the name of the Father, and of the Son, and of the Holy Ghost: teaching them to observe [obey] all things whatsoever I have commanded you: and, lo, I am with you alway, even unto the end of the world. Amen" (Matt. 28:19-20).

Peter preached on the day of Pentcost: "Then they that gladly received his word were baptized: and the same day there were added unto them about three thousand souls" (Acts 2:41). F. F. Bruce said in *Commentary on the Book of Acts*: "The idea of an unbaptized Christian is simply not entertained in the New Testament." Though baptism is not essential to salvation, it is essential to obedience.

E. We should join a Bible-preaching, Bible-believing local church and attend regularly to let people know we are on the Lord's side.

When Peter preached on the day of Pentecost, many of his hearers were saved and baptized. "And the same day there were added unto them about three thousand souls. And they continued stedfastly in the apostles' doctrine and fellowship, and in breaking of bread, and in prayers" (Acts 2:41, 42).

Not only did they become members of the church, but they were also stedfast members, attending faithfully and working for the Lord. God's Word commands: "Not forsaking the assembling of ourselves together, as the manner of some is; but exhorting one another: and so much the more, as ye see the day approaching" (Heb. 10:25).

F. We should give cheerfully to the Lord's work to let people know we are on the Lord's side.

We prove the sincerity of our love for the Lord by the way we give (II Cor. 8:8). "He which soweth sparingly shall reap also sparingly; and he which soweth bountifully shall reap also bountifully. Every man according as he purposeth in his heart, so let him give; not grudgingly, or of necessity: for God loveth a cheerful giver" (II Cor. 9:6-7).

G. In our everyday life we should let people know we are on the Lord's side. In our:

talk.
actions.
dress.
friends.
habits.
recreation.
lifestyle.

Proverbs 3:6 characterizes our lives as Christians. "In all thy ways acknowledge him. . . ."

II. Why should everyone be on the Lord's side?

A. Because of all that God has done for us. He has created us, He sustains us, He gave His Son to die for us, He gives us eternal life when we trust His Son as our personal Saviour. "Only fear the Lord, and serve him in truth with all your heart: for consider how great things he hath done for you" (I Sam. 12:24).

B. Because one day we will have to give an account to Him (Rom. 14:12).

C. Because the Lord's side is the safe side. When we are on His side, we are saved from sin, from judgment, from Hell. "He that believeth on the Son hath everlasting life: and he that believeth not the Son shall not see life; but the wrath of God abideth on him" (John 3:36).

D. Because the Lord's side is the best side. ". . . The way of transgressors is hard" (Prov. 13:15). However, Jesus promised: ". . . My yoke is easy, and my burden is light" (Matt. 11:30).

E. Because the Lord's side is the happy side. "These things have I spoken unto you, that my joy might remain in you, and that your joy might be full" (John 15:11). One Christian said: "My unhappy moments now are happier than my happy moments as a non-Christian."

F. Because the Lord's side is the useful side. When a person becomes a Christian and is on the Lord's side, he can be used in His service. He can be "a vessel unto honour, sanctified, and meet [fit] for the master's use, and prepared unto every good work" (II Tim. 2:21).

G. Because the Lord's side is the winning side. No one wants to be on the losing side: everyone wants to be on the winning side. When we are on the Lord's side we can triumphantly shout: "Thanks be to God, which giveth us the victory through our Lord Jesus Christ" (I Cor. 15:57).

III. When should we be on the Lord's side?

This is an easy question to answer. It can be answered with a three-letter word—*now*. If you are not on the Lord's side now, I pray that you will repent and believe on the Lord Jesus Christ and get on His side. ". . . Behold, now is the accepted time; behold, now is the day of salvation" (II Cor. 6:2).

If you are on the Lord's side but have not been letting people know, may you right now do what you must to let everyone know where you stand. "Now then do it. . . ." (II Sam. 3:18).

24

WHO THEN IS WILLING?

I Chronicles 29:5

David asked the congregation of Israel: "Who then is willing? . . ." Let me ask you several specific questions.

I. **Who then is willing to give his substance to the Lord?**

David had given his substance to the Lord in preparation for building the temple. He gave 3,000 talents of gold and 7,000 talents of silver (I Chron. 29:1-5), totaling millions of dollars.

Encouraged and inspired by his generous giving to the Lord, the congregation of Israel gave 5,000 talents of gold, plus 10,000 drams of gold, 10,000 talents of silver, 18,000 talents of brass, and 100,000 talents of iron, totaling many more millions of dollars (I Chron. 29:6-7).

King David and his people gave of their substance gladly and willingly because they loved the Lord. They realized that all they gave was first given to them by the Lord. David said to God: "But who am I, and what is my people, that we should be able to offer so willingly after this sort? for all things come of thee, and of thine own have we given thee" (I Chron. 29:14).

All that we have has been given to us by the Lord. Christians should give cheerfully and willingly to the Lord. God's Word teaches tithes (10% of income) and offerings (Mal. 3:8-10; Matt 23:23). According to I Corinthians 16:2 this giving should be done:

periodically. "Upon the first day of the week."

personally. "Let every one of you lay by him in store."

proportionally. "As God hath prospered him."

Are you giving God what is right, or what is left? Are you willing to give your substance to the Lord?

II. **Who then is willing to give his service to the Lord?**

The question in our text is: "And who then is willing to consecrate his service this day unto the Lord?" Our service unto the Lord should be:

"with gladness" (Ps. 100:2).

"with reverence and godly fear" (Heb. 12:28).

"fervent in spirit" (Rom. 12:11).

continuous (Dan. 6:16; Acts 26:7).

in "love" (Gal. 5:13).

"with all your heart" (I Sam 12:24). (See also Col. 3:17, 23-24.)

"in newness of spirit" (Rom. 7:6). This can also be rendered: "Under obedience to the promptings of the Spirit in newness of life."

Are you willing to give your service to the Lord?

III. **Who then is willing to give his self to the Lord?**

When you offer yourself to the Lord, at the same time He will also have your substance and service. God said that Amasiah was a man "who *willingly offered himself* unto the Lord" (II Chron. 17:16). Paul said the Macedonian Christians "first *gave their own selves* to the Lord" (II Cor. 8:5). Deborah and Barak sang: "Praise ye the Lord for the avenging of Israel, when *the people willingly offered themselves*" (Judg. 5:1-2).

God beseeches Christians to "present your bodies a living sacrifice, holy, acceptable unto God, which is your reasonable service" (Rom. 12:1).

Are you willing to give yourself to the Lord? May the prayer of Brooke Foss Westcott be your prayer also.

With bowed heads and open hearts we may offer ourselves.

We can do no more, and we dare do no less.

25

WHY PEOPLE COMMIT SUICIDE

John 5:40

An article in *U.S. News & World Report* explains: "A fresh spurt in suicides is prompting growing concern in the medical and social professions, and intensified efforts to probe the age-old puzzle of self-destruction." According to the report, "Upsurge in Suicides and in Ways to Prevent Them," 24,440 persons committed suicide in 1973 in America, a record annual total.

Suicide is rising sharply among young people and is topped only by accidental death as the most common cause of death in that age group. Hungary has the highest overall suicide rate in the world—33.1 suicides per 100,000 people. Other countries' statistics are: Czechoslovakia, 24.5; Austria, 22.3; Sweden, 22; and the United States, 11.7. The World Health Organization estimates that at least 1,000 persons commit suicide every day and that annually there are over one-half million suicides. For every suicide, there are at least eight to ten attempts.

According to Theodore Irwin in *Family Weekly*: "At least once every minute, someone in the U.S. tries to kill himself." In *Responding To Suicidal Crisis,* Doman Lum writes: "In the United States, there are at least 25,000 recorded suicides annually. The actual number may be twice that. . . . On a broad scale, 3,000,000 people in our nation have made suicide attempts."

Researchers are now interviewing "failed suicides" to develop a better picture of what drives people to suicide. Dr. Calvin J. Frederick, psychologist with the National Institute of Mental Health's Center for Studies of Crime and Delinquency, explained: "Usually, people commit suicide because they are hapless, helpless, and hopeless. Hapless, the person feels the cards are stacked against him along with 'tough luck' events. He is lonely and feels helpless to do anything about his situation, and about that time he begins to lose all hope and he is then likely to kill himself."

Dr. Joseph Hirsch, associate professor of preventive and environmental medicine at the Albert Einstein College of Medicine in New York, found that three "central features" are usually present in a suicide. Based on a five-year investigation of 32,000 suicides, he has advanced the *LAD syndrome.*

> *L* refers to *loss* and *loneliness.* Losses such as a loved one, a physical function, self-esteem, or some other privation, real or fancied. Loss is generally accompanied by a dismal feeling of loneliness.
>
> *A* refers to aggression. "This is the chief effective force behind suicide," says Dr. Hirsch.
>
> *D* refers to depression, which often causes a person to "put himself out of his misery."

Other explanations for suicide given by those who have studied the problem are: serious illness; job reversals and other work-related frustrations; hysteria; guilt feelings; excessive use of barbituates; postalcoholic withdrawal; morbidity; unhappy love affairs; the clash of individual and group demands; and the feeling of emptiness and uselessness.

Suicide has been called the saddest of human tragedies, but there is something far more tragic. Every unsaved person is spiritually dead (Eph. 2:1; I Tim. 5:6). Christ is the only source of life (John 3:36; 14:6; I John 5:12). If people would come to Christ, He would save them and give them eternal life (John 6:37; John 1:12; John 3:16, 5:24; Acts 16:31). The tragedy of all tragedies is that they will not come to Him. He laments in our text: "And ye will not come to me, that ye might have life" (John 5:40). People who do not come to Christ and receive Him as their personal Saviour commit spiritual suicide.

When I was in the pastorate, I asked the young people in the church to give me reasons why people did not come to Christ and trust Him as their personal Saviour. I compiled their responses, and here is why people commit suicide—spiritual suicide.

I. They don't realize their need.

Many unsaved people do not realize their need of Christ. I once talked to a man who said, "I have never sinned." He was a successful farmer, and it was difficult to show him that he had sinned and needed the Saviour. I showed him Romans 3:23: "For *all* have sinned, and come short of the glory of God." We also read together: "*All* we like sheep have gone astray [are lost] ; we have turned *every one* to his own way" (Isa. 53:6). Thank God, he finally saw it and recognized he was a lost sinner in need of the Saviour. Everyone needs the Saviour to get to Heaven.

II. **They think they'll have to give up everything.**

The devil has convinced people that if they become a Christian they will have to give up everything that's worthwhile and will never have any enjoyment in life. This is a lie. My life verse is: "For the Lord God is a sun and shield: the Lord will give grace and glory: *no good thing will he withhold* from them that walk uprightly" (Ps. 84:11). "He that spared not his own Son, but delivered him up for us all, how shall he not with him also *freely give us all things?*" (Rom. 8:32). ". . . The living *God, who giveth us richly all things to enjoy*" (I Tim. 6:17). Instead of giving up everything, the Christian gets everything.

III. **They are afraid of people.**

People who are unsaved are afraid of what people will say or do to them if they come to Christ. "The fear of man bringeth a snare: but whoso putteth his trust in the Lord shall be safe" (Prov. 29:25). Put your trust in the Lord and say with David: "The Lord is my light and my salvation; whom shall I fear? the Lord is the strength of my life; of whom shall I be afraid?" (Ps. 27:1). "In God have I put my trust: I will not be afraid what man can do unto me" (Ps. 56:11).

IV. **They are busy with other things.**

In the parable of the great supper in Luke 14:16-24, three people made excuses for not attending the supper—all were too busy. One said he had to view a piece of land he had bought, one said he needed to prove some oxen he had bought, and the other had married a wife. Notice what Jesus said of those who were too busy: ". . . None of those men which were bidden shall taste of my supper" (v. 24). Jesus said: "But seek ye first the kingdom of God, and his righteousness. . . ." (Matt. 6:33). It's best to put God first, not things.

V. **They say there are too many hypocrites.**

This is an excuse I have heard many times. I remind those who say this that "so then every one of us shall give account of *himself* to God" (Rom. 14:12). A person will not give an account for the hypocrite, but of himself. Yes, there are too many hypocrites, but as it has been said: "If you are hiding behind a hypocrite, he's bigger than you are."

VI. They are waiting for a feeling.

I suppose that I hear this more than any other excuse. Nowhere in the Bible does God say how you are to feel before you are saved, when you are saved, or after you are saved. The word *feel* is used only once in the New Testament (Acts 17:27), and the word *feeling* only twice (Eph. 4:19, Heb. 4:15). None of these uses relates to salvation. Trust Jesus Christ as your personal Saviour.

> Be my feelings what they will,
> Jesus is my Saviour still.

VII. They are afraid they can't hold out.

People want to be saved, but are afraid they will sin and will not be able to live the Christian life. *We* can't hold out, but if we trust Jesus Christ He will hold us. "The steps of a good man are ordered by the Lord and he delighteth in his way. Though he fall, he shall not be utterly cast down: for the Lord upholdeth him with his hand" (Ps. 37:23-24). When God saves a person, He gives him eternal life and promises he will never perish (John 10:27-29). (See Rom. 8:38-39; Phil. 1:6; II Tim. 1:12; I Peter 1:5.)

VIII. They think they have plenty of time.

People put off salvation, thinking that sometime in the future they will be saved. This is dangerous because God warns: "Boast not thyself of to morrow; for thou knowest not what a day may bring forth" (Prov. 27:1). This is the time to be saved. "Behold, now is the accepted time; behold, now is the day of salvation" (II Cor. 6:2). It is so true that "the man who plans to get saved at the eleventh hour usually dies at ten-thirty."

IX. They think they are already saved.

Millions of people in our country have joined churches and think they are saved. Past and present men of God estimate that at least 90% of the church members in America are lost. Jesus spoke of people who thought they had come to Him: "Many will say to me in that day, Lord, Lord, have we not prophesied in thy name? and in thy name have cast out devils? and in thy name done many wonderful works? and then will I profess unto them, I never knew you: depart from me, ye that work iniquity" (Matt. 7:22-23).

X. They don't know how to be saved.

At least 90% of the unsaved people do not know how to be saved. I have checked time and time again, and seldom have I found a lost person who knew what must be done to be saved. Paul gave plain directions as he preached. He went from place to place "testifying both to the Jews, and also to the Greeks, repentance toward God, and faith toward our Lord Jesus Christ" (Acts 20:21). In order to come to Christ and be saved, a person must repent (Luke 13:3; Acts 17:30; 26:20; II Peter 3:9) and believe on the Lord Jesus Christ (John 1:12; 3:16, 18, 36; 5:24; Acts 16:31; Rom 10:9, 10, 13).

My prayer for you is that you will not continue giving foolish excuses for not coming to Christ and thereby commit spiritual suicide. Instead, right now, come to Him in repentance and faith. He promises that He will take you in: ". . . Him that cometh to me I will in no wise cast out" (John 6:37).